ONE MILLION READERS

The Definitive Guide to a Nonfiction Book Marketing Strategy That Saves Time, Money, and SELLS MORE BOOKS

BONI WAGNER-STAFFORD

Contents

Read This First	vii
Introduction	ix
1. What Is a Book Marketing Strategy?	1
PART 1. GETTING STARTED	7
2. Your Objectives	9
3. Your Target Audience	17
4. Unique Selling/Service Proposition	23
5. Market Scan	27
6. Budget	35
7. Placement and Pricing	39
PART II. MESSAGES and METHODS	45
8. Messages and Methods	47
9. Web Presence	51
10. Author Photo	55
11. Social Media	63
12. Public Relations (PR)	67
13. Reader Reviews	77
14. Email Marketing	83
15. Promotional Products	85
16. Your Book Launch	89
17. Book Signing Kit	93
18. Advertising	97
PART III. TAKING ACTION	101
19. Tactical Timeline	103
20. Contact Lists	107
21. Measurement and Metrics	111
22. Book Overview	113
23. Strategy Brief	121
24. Pulling It All Together	125

Afterword	127
Acknowledgments	129
About the Author	131
Other books by Boni	133

Published by Ingenium Books Publishing

Toronto, Ontario, Canada M6P 1Z2

Copyright @2019 Boni Wagner-Stafford

All rights reserved.

www.ingeniumbooks.com

Ingenium Books supports copyright. Copyright fuels innovation and creativity, encourages diverse voices, promotes free speech, and helps create vibrant culture. Thank you for purchasing an authorized edition of this book and for complying with copyright laws by not reproducing, scanning, or distributing this book or any part of it without permission. You are supporting writers and helping ensure Ingenium Books can continue to publish nonfiction books for readers like you. You are permitted to excerpt brief quotations in a review.

ISBN:

978-1-989059-22-7 (paperback/softcover)

978-1-989059-23-4 (electronic)

978-1-989059-24-1 (audiobook)

Praise for Boni Wagner-Stafford

"*In **One Million Readers** Boni Wagner-Stafford shows indie authors how to create and implement a real-world book marketing strategy, and how this approach can help you achieve your publishing goals and sell more books. Recommended.*"
—*Joel Friedlander, TheBookDesigner.com*

Read This First

Getting Ready to Market Your Book: Your Free Marketing Strategy Template

Thank you for purchasing *One Million Readers: The Definitive Guide to a Marketing Strategy That Saves Time, Money, and Sells More Books*.

To help you get started with your book marketing strategy, I'm offering a free companion workbook that you can use to develop your own book marketing strategy.

Read the book first, then come back for the workbook. Or, get the workbook now and make notes as you read for the first time.

Download the free workbook by clicking this link, or by copying/pasting/typing it into your browser:

https://ingeniumbooks.com/one-million-readers-workbook/

At the end of the book you'll also find a link to a free example of a completed nonfiction book marketing strategy. See you there!

Introduction

Those who want to write a book believe that writing the book is the hardest part. Those who have written a book soon discover that marketing the book is actually the bigger challenge.

There is a lot of advice online — and if you filter through it all, you will find some good information. The challenge is: the volume.

There's so much advice that it is impossible to decide what to do. So much advice that, as authors, we worry how on earth we're going to heed it all. And there is so much we could do, except we have no idea how or even if it is right for us and our book.

Some people present certain book marketing activities as absolute musts, others as simple recommendations. Some of these activities — for example, Amazon ads — are so complicated they require a technical instruction book for how to read and respond to the data.

Add to that the plethora of people offering courses and how-to advice and sharing horror stories of what they tried that didn't work, and you have information overload.

It all boils down to a swirling hodgepodge of options, learning, best practices, and preferences.

The only way to get a handle on which of the gazillion possible things to do, and what is right for you and *your* book, is to craft your own marketing strategy.

Who Is This Book For?

One Million Readers is for you if:

- you're an indie author of any nonfiction genre
- you want to feel more confident about marketing your books
- you're a traditionally-published author of nonfiction who realizes you are still responsible for your own book marketing
- you don't know where to start on your book marketing journey
- you're ready to learn why creating your book marketing strategy is the most important thing you can do for your author career
- you're ready to gain power and control over your own book marketing
- you want to learn what you need to research and what information to include in your strategy
- you want to learn how to pull it all together into an actual project plan, so you never have to wonder what to do next

You are an independent author. As such, you are in business for yourself. Marketing your books and your business is a key pillar of success. You have to sell your products, which are your books. You want to increase your understanding between marketing your business and marketing your book.

One Million Readers is not for you if:

- You're looking for detailed how-to steps to build an email list.
- You want to know how to conduct keyword research and set up SEO – search engine optimization – on your author or book website.
- You want to know how to create the best lead magnets or freebies to attract people to sign up to your list.
- You want instruction on how and when to post on social media, or you want help setting up your social media accounts.
- And finally, but most importantly, *One Million Readers* is not for you if you're looking for a magic bullet that will remove from you the responsibility to lead your marketing efforts for your book.

Fiction Versus Nonfiction

While written specifically for the nonfiction author, there will still be value for you in this book if you write fiction. There are some subtle differences in nonfiction versus fiction marketing strategies, but the process and approach are the same. The examples included throughout *One Million Readers* are all nonfiction. If you're a fiction author and you don't think this is appropriate for you, you probably want to stop reading now and search for another resource.

Why Listen to Me?

My experience with marketing, communications, and public relations strategies is built on a foundation of more than a dozen years in journalism, and then another decade crafting, leading, and implementing communications strategies for high profile provincial government ministries in Ontario, Canada .

The first communications strategy I wrote was for the Ontario government's modernization of its Credit Union & Caisse Populaires Act. The work involved consultations with industry and other regulatory bodies (e.g. The Financial Services Commission of Ontario), seeking input on proposed changes to the legislation, working with the legislature on introduction of the amendments, and researching related avenues. My responsibility was to write the plan for how the Ontario government was going to communicate amendments to disparate audiences: the finance industry as a whole, small credit union operators, large chain-type players, lobbyists, and consumers.

I was also responsible for communications strategies for Ontario's work on a Single Securities Regulator for Canada, legislative and regulatory work related to real estate brokers and agents, tourism industry revitalization, sales tax harmonization, modernization of libraries and museums, and more. I participated on government-wide marketing initiatives designed to drive more tourist traffic to the province's tourist and cultural destinations, and to attract international film and television business.

It is this experience we leverage to bring a robust approach to our book marketing strategies at Ingenium Books, and it is this experience that informs the following advice for how you can prepare your own impactful and significant book marketing strategy.

The common denominators with all of those communications strategies, and the book marketing strategy work we do at Ingenium Books include building knowledge about:

- what you're trying to achieve
- what you've got that's different
- what's happening in the broader environment
- who you need to reach
- what you want your audience to do
- how you're going to help your audience do it

How to Use the Information in This Book

You'll begin with an overview of what a book marketing strategy is, and together we'll take a walk through the structure so you can build a picture in your mind of the end product.

Then the material follows the order in which you will actually do the work: ***Part I, Getting Started***, covers the elements you can begin before you even start to write your book. By thinking about the elements covered in Part I, you'll help ensure you create the right content for the right audience and that you've identified the right audience for the book you're creating.

In ***Part II, Messages & Methods***, you'll find all the elements you will want to consider that cover what you are going to say in your marketing efforts and what method you're going to use to deliver your message.

Part III, Taking Action, is where the rubber hits the road. You'll learn how to create your tactical timeline and build out the action steps so you have a clear map to follow. You'll get some tips for how to set up tracking for your measurement and metrics, so you know what's working and what to tweak. And it is here where you'll write the materials that live at the top of the strategy: the book overview and the strategy brief.

Within each section you'll see that I've presented information following the *what, why,* and *how* format. This will help you learn **what** a particular component is, understand **why** it is important, and finally **how** you can pull it together for your own book marketing strategy.

If you're the type of author who likes to plan your book with a detailed outline first, and then write in a linear fashion, writing chapter one before you start on chapter two, the approach recommended in *One Million Readers* might feel a little uncomfortable.

That's because the first pieces you must tackle are not the first elements of your finished marketing strategy.

Let's dive in.

1

What Is a Book Marketing Strategy?

Your book marketing strategy addresses *why* you've written your book, *why* the marketing strategy exists, and *what* you're going to do to market your book.

It is the plan that helps you drive toward your goals. It becomes your point of reference when you say, "What should I be doing today to market my book?" It will provide the answer to that question.

It's a document that will build up your confidence and comfort with talking to all kinds of people about your book, whether you're speaking to the next buyer of your book(s), a literary agent, a traditional publisher, or a documentary or television producer. It will help you discuss your book in a business-like and objective fashion. It will help you take a bird's eye view of your book, where it fits in the marketplace, whose problem it solves and how it will help solve that problem.

There's a marketing component to every business plan. The book marketing strategy serves a similar purpose — providing impetus for thought and planning when and how you're going to sell your services, wares, or intellectual property (that's your book). It plays a critical role in helping you think about your book as though it was the key product in your business. It's the exercise that gives you a leg up.

What a book marketing strategy will not do, no matter how innovative, good, or thorough, is make up for an inferior product. Your manuscript must be the best it can possibly be, which means professionally edited and proofread. Your neighbour or best friend who loves to read does not count. Your book cover must be professionally designed, meaning unless you are a designer you do not want a do-it-yourself cover. Before you invest time and money in building a marketing strategy, be sure you've invested the right amount of time and money into these foundational elements of your book.

Strategy Components

Before we dive into the meat of the how-to sections, let's look at the recommended structure for your completed book marketing strategy.

You'll organize your content into three sections:

1. Groundwork
2. Messages & Methods
3. Mechanics

Here's a look at the table of contents for a good book marketing strategy.

Section 1. The Groundwork
Book Overview
Strategy Brief
Market Scan
Objectives
Target Audience
Unique Selling Proposition (USP)
Placement and Distribution
Section 2. Messages & Methods

Web Presence
Author Photo
Social Media
Public Relations (PR)
Reader Reviews
Email Marketing
Promotional Products
Book Launch
Book Signing Kit
Section 3. Mechanics
Tactical Timeline
Contact Lists
Measurement and Metrics

Marketing Versus Promotion

There is a difference between marketing and promotion.

Marketing is everything about you and your books.

Promotion is what you do when you want to sell your book.

You can engage in marketing without promotion, for example when you wish to raise your author profile but don't necessarily set out to sell books.

You can engage in promotion without marketing, for example when you have something to sell but aren't necessarily worried about the connection to your author brand.

For our author business and our books, marketing activities are necessary to build profile, author brand awareness, and connections. Promotion is far more effective after you've built awareness with your audience. You don't want to say, "buy me" before you say, "get to know me."

By following the approach in *One Million Readers*, you will be covering both marketing and promotion. You'll get a good sense of where the two intersect, where one supports the other, and how to leverage each to achieve the best possible results.

Creating Your Own Book Marketing Strategy Versus Hiring Help

You might wonder why you'd want to create your book marketing strategy yourself when there are others out there happy to take your money in exchange for doing one for you?

Many of the professional book marketing strategy services out there are very good. This might be an option for you to consider. However, here are four reasons you'll benefit from putting in the time and effort required to build your strategy yourself.

1. **Knowledge.** There's nothing more empowering than digging in to do the research, sorting through the rationale, and really getting to know what's behind the curtains of your very own book marketing strategy.
2. **Confidence.** Knowledge breeds confidence, and that means you'll have an easier time speaking to others about your book and engaging with potential readers and influencers. You'll benefit from confidence in knowing not only what you're doing, but why and how.
3. **Clarity.** You'll know exactly where you're going and how you're going to get there. You'll have created for yourself a marketing roadmap that you can follow from the beginning. No more driving in the dark without headlights. And this is a map you'll keep on referencing, over and over. It will steer your marketing approach, your content, your timing, your social media.
4. **Cost.** These strategies are big, long, and detailed, and hiring someone to produce a really good one can be pricey.

Even if you do decide to hire someone else to create your book marketing strategy, by reading *One Million Readers* first, you will have a much better understanding of the market forces at play. You'll know and appreciate the environment into which you are launching your book. And you'll be able to collaborate with your chosen strategist to achieve better results in the end.

Too many book marketing services or tools would have you adopting a zoom-lens look at tactics, one after the other. I agree there is value in focus, however what I advocate is the connection to your purpose, your book's purpose, and where you as author and your book fit in the broader environment. It is this context that will:

- set you up for a much more efficient book marketing exercise
- help you decide which tactics make the most sense
- deepen your awareness of the variables in the market so you know how, where, and when to best present your book to buyers

By creating your own book marketing strategy, you'll see, understand, and connect the dots in the big picture first. You'll end up with a plan of action that aligns with your purpose for writing the book. You'll chart a course leading to the achievement of your goals, whether they include selling 2,000 copies, reaching one million readers, or achieving bestseller status in one or more categories.

PART 1. GETTING STARTED

2

Your Objectives

The very first thing you want to nail are the marketing objectives for your book. You're likely familiar with objectives and the key role they play in any business (or personal) endeavour.

The many authors that discount, overlook, or dismiss setting objectives for their books as irrelevant miss out on the key strategic link that objectives provide between dreams and reality.

What Are Objectives?

The objectives are the pillars for everything you plan and do related to the marketing of your book. It's your why, your goals, your dreams, all wrapped up into an action-focused package.

Objectives describe exactly what you want to achieve through your marketing approach. Here's an example using a special vacation as an analogy.

Your objective for the vacation might be to unwind, relax, and recharge your batteries. Or, it might be to experience a thrilling physical adventure, such as climbing Mount Everest, rowing across the Atlantic, or some other experience where you'll push yourself beyond your current boundaries.

Understanding your objectives for your vacation will help you:

- Choose the location. A five-star beach resort will be perfect for the relaxation objective but not so much for the adventure.
- Decide how you'll get there. A direct flight, perhaps in first class, will be perfect for the relaxing beach vacation. Backpacking, hitchhiking, or train might allow you to experience more of the region you're visiting for your adventure vacation.
- How much money you'll spend in order to meet your vacation objectives.

It's the same thing with the objectives for your book marketing strategy.

Why Determine Objectives Before You Begin

Your objectives are the pillars for everything you plan and do related to the marketing of your book. In fact, ideally you will have examined your objectives for the book early in the writing process, as objectives will affect everything including your content, tone, design, and length.

Your objectives are going to help you decide everything you do to market your book and yourself as an author. They will be objectives unique to you and your book.

Before you can articulate your marketing objectives, you need to have solid bigger-picture objectives for why you wrote the book in the first place. Is your objective to support yourself and make a decent living with your writing? Create a marketing hook that drives potential clients and customers to your business? Simply to tell that important story so family and friends have a chance to learn from it?

How to Set Book Marketing Objectives

How do you figure out what your marketing objectives are? It might be easy. You might know them without doing any work at all. If you don't know them, or even if you think you do, think hard and dig deep so that you can get specific.

In general, the objectives of most authors will fall into these three broad categories: awareness, engagement, and book sales. Start by drilling down into each of these categories. Here's what you need to ask:

AWARENESS:

- What kind of awareness do you want to raise? Is it for you as an author? For your book, or for the subject you're writing about? All of the above?
- Who is it that needs to be more aware?
- Is this awareness a prerequisite to some change you're advocating?

ENGAGEMENT:

- Do you want to speak at conferences and events?
- Do you want to engage with readers by doing book readings or signings?
- Do you want to speak at schools, libraries, or business meetings?
- Do you want to build an online community of loyal readers, or build an engaged email list of readers who

will want to buy your next book, and the one after that?

BOOK SALES:

- How many books do you want to sell? Be realistic and also bold in your answer to this one. Don't say two, but also probably don't say two million. How do you know what's a realistic goal? It depends on the genre; it depends on the marketing strategy; it depends on the quality; it depends on your marketing budget; and it depends on whether you have a team or you're marketing solo.
- Research how other books are selling in your genre. Use tools like KDP Rocket (https://publisherrocket.com/), or KDSpy (https://www.kdspy.com/), or even start with a simple Google search. My search using the term, "global book sales by genre," led me to https://www.statista.com/statistics/322187/book-genres-revenue/ where, for example, I re-discovered that more money is spent buying business books than all fiction categories combined.
- Manually search on Amazon and other search engines (though both KDP Rocket and KDSpy source Amazon data, so if you have access to those tools then your job is a little easier). Get a good sense of what the bestsellers in your genre are doing.

Be realistic about your chances but set yourself a stretch goal. Make it something that's going to make you proud once you've achieved it.

Why Awareness Always Comes First

Let's say, for example, that an author's main objective at the start of our process is to get hired for speaking engagements. In this case, an author may say they don't really care about becoming well known and they don't care that much about book sales.

What has to be in place before they receive offers to speak at conferences and events? The person making the offer must be *aware* that the author and the book exist. Therefore, awareness must come first. No one will hire an author they don't know about.

We could leave this author's marketing strategy with those two objectives: raise awareness and get hired for speaking gigs. However, book sales play a key role.

Getting hired for speaking gigs — the author's number one objective — requires awareness on the front end and book sales for credibility on the back end. It's great if Sam the Conference Organizer finds out there's an author who has written a book about the specific topic the conference wants to address. It's better, by far, if there is evidence that people are actually buying the author's book. If there's demand for the book, Sam knows there will be an engaged and interested audience at his conference.

It's this third pillar, book sales, that is the *most* common objective for *most* authors. Including tactics in your marketing strategy around awareness is critical for achieving book sales: readers are less likely to buy a book from an author they've never heard about.

General Versus Specific

At Ingenium Books, crafting marketing strategies on behalf of authors is a collaborative effort. We ask authors to complete a series of questionnaires and we have one or more conversations to get them thinking and to be sure we can extract and articulate clear and authentic objectives.

In this collaborative process, however, most authors do not show up with the level of specificity we want them to reach for, in particular around the objectives. Broad objectives are better than no objectives, but specific objectives are far better than broad objectives.

So, we work at that.

Sheila and Joe

Sheila has written a book about her business. Joe has written a memoir about his family's story. Because their overall objectives (their why) for writing the book in the first place are different, their marketing objectives are going to be different too, even though they will each have objectives in the broad categories of awareness, engagement, and book sales.

Your Objectives • 15

COMPARING THE OBJECTIVES

SHEILA'S BUSINESS BOOK

JOE'S MEMOIR

AWARENESS

Increase book, authorship, and business awareness

Leave a legacy for children and family.

Become well known locally, regionally, nationally

Every living relative owns the book

ENGAGEMENT

Invited to speak 2xconferences/year

5-10 geneology groups post review

200% increase in web traffic and leads

Invited to speak to local & regional groups dealing with main book topics

Reviewed by high-profile book reviewers

BOOK SALES

Sell 2000 copies in 12 months

Sell 250 copies in 12 months

50 Amazon reviews in 3 months

10 Amazon reviews in 3 months

Sell 500 copies/year x 2 years

Sell 25 copies/year x 2 years

IF YOU FAIL TO NAIL YOUR OBJECTIVES BEFORE YOU BEGIN TO work on the rest of your book marketing plan, you risk including too many irrelevant tactics or not enough of the right ones. And you will have a harder time achieving the objectives you set.

3

Your Target Audience

Think of a target audience as your market. It includes your readers, of course, and it also includes influencers: those people or organizations that can help you reach more readers.

For the purposes of *writing* your book, it's your audience of ideal readers that you most need to consider. For your book marketing strategy and follow-on tactics, you'll want to think more broadly and include influencers.

Your reader is who you've written your book for. You want to have a clear understanding of who your ideal reader is before you even start writing. (If you've already finished your manuscript and you're just thinking about your reader now, this is a case of better late than never.)

Let's use the example of Jamie Sussel Turner's book, *Less Stress Life: How I Went from Crazed to Calm and You Can Too*. Having had a hand in the development of this manuscript, I know that the target reader for *Less Stress Life* is a person like Jean. Jean is a divorced career woman in her mid-forties who is feeling the crush at the intersection between a demanding job, a busy household, teenage kids considering university, and aging parents.

Your reader is a person you can name and describe who will benefit from your book and its solutions to their biggest problems.

Influencers, from the perspective of your marketing strategy, are different. These are people who represent a route to your reader. They may have access to multiple readers and hold a position of influence. But they're not necessarily going to be a reader, per se, nor are they necessarily going to buy your book. Members of the media would fall into this category, as well as podcasters with a large following. Other possible influencers include teachers who would recommend the book to their students, counsellors and coaches who would recommend the book to their clients, and conference organizers responsible for building the content of their programs.

Why Define These Audiences?

When you have done the work of drilling down to the specifics of who your ideal reader is and who your influencers are, you will be able to identify where you'll find them, what their preferences for communication are, and how to connect with them.

Identify Your Reader

It's all about balance. If you try to reach everyone you will likely appeal to no one, but if only a handful of people meet all your criteria, you've needlessly gone too far.

It's often more difficult to define your ideal reader, and many books will have more than one, so we'll start there. To do this you'll begin by asking a number of questions in the categories of the demographics, the personal, values and goals, information sources, and pain points and challenges.

THE DEMOGRAPHICS:

1. How old are your readers? What's their gender and marital status? A twenty-year-old single man is going to respond differently to marketing methods than a fifty-year-old married woman. Both might be an ideal reader of your book and knowing who they are is key to effectively marketing to them.
2. Where do they live? Knowing this will help you devise location-based marketing campaigns. It can help you figure out where to target traditional marketing methods. It will also provide insight into their likely political leanings: if we take the United States as an example, a reader who lives on a ranch in the Midwest is likely to have different tastes in books and how to consume them than the one who lives in a high-rise in downtown San Francisco. Be careful with geographic generalities though. There is information there that needs to be verified before you make assumptions — or perhaps your reader is the exception to the rule.
3. What is their level of education? For example, do they have a basic high-school education, or do they have a PhD?
4. What industry do they work in? Are you aiming your books at certain professionals? For example, if your book is about an employee evaluation tool, you might want to target people who work in human resources.
5. How much do they earn? In addition to insight into where they might find your book, e.g. on loan from the library, digitally via their new e-reader, or the brand-new glossy hardcover, it will also inform your pricing strategy. Pricing is an important factor in how well your book will sell. More on pricing later in chapter 7, *Placement and Pricing*.

THE PERSONAL:

1. How do they spend their free time? As with knowing what industry your reader works in, knowing how they spend their free time can help you position your book and tailor your marketing campaign accordingly.
2. How do they think? Here you need to consider factors like personality type, values and attitudes, lifestyle, and behaviour.
3. What are their hopes and dreams? Especially for nonfiction, being able to identify the hopes and dreams of your reader is going to help you position your book as a way to help them realize those hopes and dreams.
4. What makes them laugh? Using humour is a great way to market your books. However, you need to know the kind of humour your audience will respond to or you may risk alienating them instead.
5. Who are their idols? Who would be considered an influencer in their network? Are they fans of a famous radical talk show host? Do they swoon over a particular big-screen actor? Do they avidly follow and consume everything and anything from a particular social media star? The answers to these questions can lead to innovative avenues to get you and your book in front of them.

VALUES AND GOALS:

1. What are the values and beliefs that guide your readers every day?

2. What is it that your readers want to achieve in their personal lives or in business?
3. What problems are they looking to solve and how can your book help them solve those problems?

INFORMATION SOURCES:

1. How and where do your readers get their information? Do they get it primarily through social media or through online articles, for example? Do they prefer traditional sources like newspapers, magazines, or word of mouth? Which newspapers, magazines, and websites are their favourites? Do they respond better to advertising on billboards, in the media, on public transit, or direct marketing campaigns?
2. How do your readers communicate? Knowing whether they prefer email, face-to-face interaction, phone calls, posts on social media, and so on will help you determine the best way to market your book to them.
3. What pushes your readers to buy books? Look at what influences them to make that purchase and also what might prevent them from buying your book.
4. What other books has your reader already bought and read? You need to know this so you can find the angle that makes your book special, that makes your book the one they should buy.

PAIN POINTS AND CHALLENGES:

1. What challenges does your reader face and what causes them? What's the emotional toll of these challenges? Your book might address some of these already. Otherwise, knowing the challenges your target audience faces can help you decide what to focus on in your book and in your marketing.
2. How can your book help alleviate these pain points and challenges?
3. What would be their biggest objections to buying your book? You need to know this so that you can help them overcome those objections and buy your book.

Identifying Your Influencers

Identifying your influencers is always going to involve a trip back to review the objectives discussed in chapter 2, *Your Objectives*. Consider the example of an author whose primary objective is to secure four high-profile speaking engagements this year. In her case, the people who work for those conferences, who hire the keynote speakers and workshop trainers, are in the bulls-eye of her influencer audience. Remember that reaching your influencers is a different exercise than reaching readers directly.

4

Unique Selling/Service Proposition

Your unique selling (or service) proposition, or USP, is what sets you and/or your book apart in the competitive marketplace. With a USP, you will be better able to target your marketing and sales efforts.

Let's talk about some of the ways other businesses leverage their USPs in their marketing. You can do this by looking at what other companies are saying and doing in their marketing messages. You'll find most savvy companies will sell an experience, or a feeling, not just their products or services.

Starbucks sells a welcoming and friendly environment. Walmart sells bargains. Costco sells value. Neal's Yard Remedies sells a clean, healthy environment. Ingenium Books, our author services publishing company, sells the creation and expression of ideas.

Think of the USP for your book as the thing that sets your book apart from all the others in the category and/or genre. It's the hook that you can hang your marketing strategy on. Any business, whether they sell widgets or books, can look to the "four P's" of marketing (product, price, place, promotion) to find and focus on their USP.

How to Identify Your USP

Start by looking at what other businesses and other successful authors in your genre are doing with their USPs. And you should be able to tell whether they've done the work to set themselves up with one.

If your book is related to your business, expect an overlapping USP between the two. If you've written a self-help book, or a memoir, your USP is likely going to be something related to you, as author, since your perspective on the self-help advice you're offering is going to be linked to your unique personal experience and expertise.

If you get stumped when trying to describe the USP for your book, back up and focus on the thing you know best: you. Make your USP about you as the author — there is no other *you* out there, so it's a matter of finding that aspect of unique that helps you tell readers and influencers why you are their author and your books are for them.

This makes the most sense when you consider that regardless of the genre or topic of your book, your readers will get to know you over the course of the read. Think about your content from that perspective: what have you revealed about yourself, your journey, and your experience that you can turn into your USP? What is it about you that made it possible for you to write *that* book, at *this* time?

Here's another example from Ingenium Books' author Yvonne Caputo. Yvonne is a psychologist, former teacher, and former HR executive who has written *Flying With Dad*, a memoir about the things she learned about her father and his WWII experiences in the last few years before he died. Yvonne was finally able to build the relationship with her father that she had always wanted — through the research and writing of the book. Yvonne's USP is *interpersonal insights*. She's the only one who brings the experience and perspective on the trajectory of a relationship with her dad that had a rough beginning and a poignant end.

Every author, and every book, has a USP. Once you discover yours, embrace it. Talk about it and experiment with how you'd incorporate the concept of the USP into your promotional materials.

5

Market Scan

The market scan looks at what is happening externally that relates to the genre, subject, or focus of your book and explores why readers will want to buy your book.

In a market scan you'll look at how books in your genre are selling, who the successfully-selling authors are, where your genre stacks up in overall book sales, and what formats sell best and worst in your genre. It's also where you'll take a look at the broader environment to see what is happening in the world relative to your genre and the subject areas within your book.

Why Conduct a Market Scan?

Looking at both the market and the environment helps orient you to the broader forces at work on your readers. It's about more than who your readers are or where you're going to find them. It is going to help you answer these questions:

- Why will readers want to buy your book?
- Why now?
- What opportunities are there for you to get in front

of the reader that you may not have thought of had you not done this piece of work?
- What else is happening in the world that could impact your book's success?

Here's how to conduct your market scan.

Competitors

Start the market scan by looking at competitors. This will give you all sorts of information, from ideas on cover design, based on ones you see that you like and that you think are effective, what sorts of covers readers in the genre seem to prefer (checking sales rank), what titles work or don't work, what are the average, high and low prices, what categories are being used by competitors, and which categories might hold some opportunity.

To do this, check Amazon, Goodreads, and also perform a straight Google search. Sometimes a competitor book will pop up in Google that either isn't on one of the other platforms, or that you somehow missed.

Next, search by general subject matter and dig around a little deeper into the categories. See what books you find listed there. Take screen shots of the covers and put them into a table so you can create a grid to see them all together without all the competing text. (I just use a simple Word or Google doc table for this.) Create a spreadsheet that includes the title, author, publish date, publisher, number of reviews and the average rating, and price. If you have KDP Rocket, or KDSpy, you will also be able to tell average daily and monthly sales for competitor titles and categories.

Retail Data

If you're a prolific writer, you may not need to do this exercise every time. However, I strongly recommend you do this work at least once per year. Meaning, if you are publishing three books per year, you probably only have to check the retail data after every third book.

If you're wondering why you should care about how many books are selling in which country and in which genre, here's a hypothetical parallel example related to a new invention. Imagine you have a great idea for a new product that you think is going to revolutionize the way people tie their shoes. You would not invest in the time to patent, prototype, manufacture, and market this new product before you did some research into the broader market. What is the shoe sales industry worth? How many pairs of shoes does the average person buy over his or her lifetime, in the US? Canada? India? What are the most common types of shoe-fastener out there and what's the history? What are the problems with the way people tie their shoes now? Is anyone else already selling what you think you've invented? Has anyone else written a book about this?

It's the same with your book. You want to build at least a bit of knowledge about the industry and economic environment into which you are launching your book, which is your product.

Check sources like Statista for US books sales and publishing industry data and, depending on the genre, you might head over to the OECD (Organization for Economic Cooperation and Development) website, check Statistics Canada, and try to find aggregated sales figures for trade and self-published books across all genres. And then there's Bookstat, which is the company spun out of the formerly anonymous "Data Guy" quarterly author earnings reports that seemed to dig deeper into the data than anyone else was able to do.

Environment

The "environment" is the socio-economic climate into which you want to release your book. Look for news stories that focus on the topic of your book. Watch for governmental statements or initiatives that might be related to your subject area. Think about economic factors and social, technological, or leisure trends, and look at these locally, regionally, nationally, and globally.

- If you're writing a book about addiction, you'd look for statistics about how many people are struggling with addiction. You'd also look at how society and the media treat addiction-related themes, such as the opioid crisis, or celebrities who have opened up about their own struggles with addiction.
- If you've written a science fiction book that, for example, talks about futuristic biometric technology, you'd do enough additional research so that you know what's happening with the technology at the moment, and you'll look at what that tells you about who's interested in that subject matter and what some of the issues are.

You've likely done much of this research in the course of writing your book. However, you might have been writing this book for the last two or three years. A lot can change in between your initial research of the subject and now, when you're ready to plan your marketing.

'Flying with Dad' Environmental Scan

Let's revisit Yvonne Caputo again and her book *Flying with Dad*. Here is the narrative treatment of the environmental scan section for Yvonne Caputo's memoir:

> The anniversaries of a number of significant
> World War events occur in 2018 and 2019.
> There will be widespread commemorative

events in the UK in November of 2018 to mark the 100th anniversary of the end of WWI. The 75th anniversary of the D-Day invasion of Europe will be commemorated around the world in 2019.

To this day, there are strong memories of the one-and-a-half million American GIs who landed in Britain – the "Friendly Invasion" – and their cultural influence. According to statistics from the US Department of Veterans Affairs, 558,000 of the sixteen million Americans who served in World War II were still alive in 2017.

In popular culture, recent films such as *Churchill* and *Dunkirk* add to the environment of remembering war events. Additionally, the widespread occurrence of post-traumatic stress disorder or PTSD and the healing power of storytelling are related to one of the aspects of the book.

The heightened awareness of military history and those who fought make it an ideal time for the release of **Flying with Dad.**

It might seem obvious, but you'd be surprised how clarifying it can be to do this work with purpose, and how it can help you see exactly who to target with your marketing and why. For *Flying with Dad*, we immediately identified globally significant events that would raise the profile of one of the main subjects and settings in Caputo's book: her father's experience as a navigator flying B-24 bombers out of the base at Rackheath, England during WWII. The people that are interested in, attending, and following these events are likely to be more interested in buying and reading *Flying with Dad*.

Nonfiction Business Book Environmental Scan

Here's another example from a nonfiction business book about meeting facilitation where we've used more of a statistical, rather than narrative, approach to presenting the information.

> Attentiv.com's deep dive into American meeting statistics reveals the need for meeting facilitation experts like you:
> * There are eleven million meetings per day in the US. That's 220 million every month or over a billion each year.
> * The average salary cost of a meeting is $338 (not including CEO salary – those meetings can cost $20k).
> * Meetings conducted without a pre-planned agenda: 63 percent.
> * Meetings that are staff, task force, and information sharing: 88 percent.
> * Meeting participants say 33 percent of meeting time is unproductive.
> * The biggest complaints about meetings: inconclusive/no decisions made, poorly organized, dominated by a few people.
> * The most common meeting length: thirty-one to sixty minutes.
> * The Wall Street Journal reports that 73 percent of meetings involve just two to four people.
> * The number of employees that waste up to thirty minutes a day simply looking for a meeting space: 40 percent.
> * Following a detailed agenda can reduce meeting times up to 80 percent, yet only 37 percent of US meetings use an agenda.

All of this points to the importance and huge cost savings of running efficient meetings. Thus, your unique insights are valuable for any business that has more than a few employees.

In this case, a business book about meeting facilitation, it makes sense to review and include in your marketing strategy statistics on how many meetings there are every day, every month, what the average cost of a meeting is, and so on. Some of these statistics may already be included in the content of the book, some may not. Some of the statistics may get incorporated into other marketing materials, such as speeches or presentations. It makes it easier to make the case for why the book is relevant and how it can help solve the reader's problem.

6

Budget

Your budget for book marketing is just like any other budget: it's a summary of how much money you have available and how you'll spend it.

Why Create a Book Marketing Budget?

Your budget will determine how you will market your book. It guides your decisions about which marketing activities to focus on. If you have lots of money available for marketing, the sky may be your limit with how you choose to market your book. That's not the case for most indie authors.

Drawing up a budget will help you determine how much money you need for marketing. If you know how much you need, you can make plans to get the money together.

Another advantage of having a detailed budget is that it makes it easier to adjust your marketing strategy when your financial situation changes, or when your measurement and metrics show that a certain aspect of your strategy is working much better than another. You can see at a glance where you can save or where you can spend more.

If you don't have much money to spend on things like paid advertisements, promotional materials, or a paid PR professional, you'll want to craft a strategy that allows you to focus on what you can afford.

If you want to try to set a zero budget for marketing your book, good luck. Some of the things you will want to do to promote and sell your book are going to cost you a least a little bit.

How to Create Your Budget

Start by listing every activity that you expect will require out-of-pocket spending. Then do your research. Don't just assume costs: get real numbers. For most you can do an online search to get a ballpark figure. Ask for quotes from service providers to get an idea of the market rate in your area. This will also reveal options for service providers, in the event that later you decide to contract out some of your marketing activities.

Say, for example, you want a professional website for your book. How much does a web designer charge? And how much would it cost to buy a domain name? How much would you need to pay per month to a web hosting company to host your website? You'd also need to think about all the other details, like how much you'll pay to license the images for the site, or to get help with your SEO (search engine optimization.)

When you consider the cost of each activity, list every little detail. Every phone call you make, for instance, costs money. So does the Internet you use for emails, social media, research, and your website. The amounts may seem insignificant, but all these little costs add up. If you budget for everything, there won't be surprises once you put your marketing plan into action. And, you'll have a head start on your taxes. Bonus.

Developing your marketing budget is a two-stage process: you'll start pulling the information together now, at the front-end of your planning, and then once you've completed all other elements of your strategy, review your budget again and make any necessary adjustments to both the budget and your planned marketing activities.

7

Placement and Pricing

Placement is where you are going to "place" your books to make them accessible and available for readers to buy. Unless your book requires custom stitching or an unusual size, or has a lot of full-colour photos, you're likely going to want to choose print-on-demand (POD) placement and distribution options. As mentioned earlier, placement (which I sometimes call distribution, though distribution is technically your route to placement) is about choosing where readers will find and buy your book, such as Amazon KDP, IngramSpark, Audible/ACX or Findaway, and Draft2Digital.

Why Plan Your Placement and Pricing?

There are many more options for you and your book than simply uploading to Amazon. Thinking about your placement and how you are going to reach readers, perhaps readers around the globe, is key to helping you realize your marketing objectives. And pricing is important because you don't want to undervalue your book, and you don't want to overprice it out of the range of what readers will expect to pay based on how your competitors have priced similar books.

How to Plan Placement

I agree with the formal recommendation from the Alliance of Independent Authors (ALLi): go 'wide', ensuring your book is available across all retailers and not just Amazon, even though Amazon is a behemoth and will likely be a major source of your royalties, at least at the beginning. Going wide means being careful not to sign on for any exclusivity agreements despite the tantalizing offers of higher royalties.

However, going wide may not be right for you and your book. Depending on whether you're new to the game and your objectives for your book marketing, it may make more sense for you to do KU (KDP Unlimited), which means not selling your book anywhere but Amazon KDP, at least for ninety days. Only you can decide.

There are other distribution and placement options, but here are the main ones you want to consider and include in your book marketing strategy.

1. Amazon/KDP: for Kindle e-book
2. Ingram Spark: for hardcover and paperback distribution to Amazon and beyond
3. Draft2Digital or Smashwords: for all other e-book platforms (except Kobo)
4. Kobo: go direct to Kobo to get your book onto an e-book platform that is popular with Canadians

Advantages of KDP

KDP offers fast and good distribution through Amazon, fast and affordable shipping to US customers, is great for shipping "review copies" to North American-based bloggers and/or for giveaways like on Goodreads.

. . .

Advantages of IngramSpark

Ingram Spark offers distribution and access to all bookstores and libraries, many of whom refuse to order from Amazon. It offers fast and affordable shipping to international customers and is great for the copies you want to send as samples to bookstores or for autographed copies.

You'll be able to place orders directly from either KDP or Ingram Spark, meaning you don't have to deal with actual inventory or schlepping books to and from the post office.

What About Book Stores?

While Ingram Spark's distribution model helps get your book in front of book stores and libraries so they can choose to stock, or at least provide an ordering option for customers who want your book, there is no reason you couldn't approach local bookstores and ask if they would carry your book.

If you are interested in learning more about how, read Debbie Young's book, written and published on behalf of the Alliance of Independent Authors (ALLi), called "How to Get Your Self-Published Book into Bookstores," available for sale at most online book retailers. (ALLi members can get the book for free through their member portal. Want to join ALLi? Highly recommended. Join via this link: http://bit.ly/JoinALLI.)

How to Set Pricing

First, look back at the competitor scan described in chapter 5, *Market Scan*. You'll recall the recommendation that you make note of the prices set for your competitor books. You'll want to take a closer look at the prices for all formats. What's the highest price? The lowest? Note the prices of the top sellers in each relevant category. Where in that price range do you think your readers will be most interested in buying your book? There are a few other issues here to discuss.

. . .

Royalties

When you set up your distributor account on Amazon KDP, for example, and you reach the pricing area, you'll be faced with pricing choices based on what royalty percentage you want. Setting the price of an e-book below $2.99US and above $9.99US will earn you a 35 percent royalty. But, if you set the price between $2.99 and $9.99, you'll earn a whopping 70 percent. But who is this choice about? Setting price based on the royalty amounts is about *you*. Marketing your book is about *your reader*. Of course, the royalty percentage is going to be a factor for you. Consciously put the royalty fees aside when you're setting your pricing strategy and think instead only of the reader. That means asking these questions:

- What price is my reader going to expect to pay?
- What are they going to want to pay?
- What message might my price send to the reader about my book? If it's free, or $.99, does it send the message that the book is no good? If it's priced at the top of the range, does it send the message that it's packed with more value than the competitors?

The answers to these questions are what you want to pay attention to when setting the price of your book.

What About Free?

Unless you're including a free promotion of your e-book for a limited time, or it's a conscious strategy with the first book in a series set to free to encourage read-throughs, setting your book's price at free is never a good idea. You decide, of course. To me, free sends the wrong message about self-published books (that they're not worth anything). It is a sign that an author doesn't know how else to market his book, so setting the price to free seems like the only thing he can do to generate "sales." This won't be you, because you're in the process of learning how to create a powerful marketing strategy and price is not the only tool in your kit.

PART II. MESSAGES and METHODS

8

Messages and Methods

Your message is all about what you're going to say, and your methods are the products that will help you say it. You know you have something to say, or you wouldn't have written your book, right? Now it's time to decide what you're going to use your voice to say as you *market* your book: these become your 'messages.'

Your messages will incorporate your USP, content from your back cover copy and your sales page, content from your book, as well as perhaps information about your experience leading up to and through the writing of the book.

The methods could include articles, opinion pieces, blogs, social media content, images, videos, media releases.

Why Plan Your Messages and Methods?

You'll know by now I'm a fan of planning for success. If you fail to plan your messages and methods, you may find yourself churning out content without any direction or purpose, and without knowing if you can expect real benefits. So, articulating a summary of your messages and the methods you'll use to disseminate them lets you focus on those pieces of content that are going to be most helpful in achieving your objectives. In other words, this section becomes your content roadmap.

How to Plan Your Messages and Methods

Think about your messages and methods in three tiers.

- **Tier one** is for your big ideas. Here's where you write down between two and four broad topics. For inspiration, look to your book's introduction, and the sections of your book. Each of these can likely be summarized or reworked into these methods: essays, opinion pieces, how-to articles, and speeches.
- **Tier two** is for specific topics from your book. Tier two messages can be crafted from chapter summaries or they can address individual points. The methods for your tier two messages will include guest blog posts or articles for your online influencer properties —these are the places your target readers go to get their information—and a series of blog posts for your own website, if you have one.
- **Tier three** is for paragraph and sentence-level detail. You'll review what you've come up with in the first two tiers and then pull specific bits out to create a series of social posts, promotional messages about your book, email nurturing sequences for your email list, and perhaps even some Q&As for your website or for interactions with reader fans.

Create a document with three sections, one for each tier. Then, review your book's table of contents and note the big ideas, the topics, and then build out the detail from that. Maintain this as a working document while you complete the rest of your marketing strategy, tweaking and honing and adding and removing items as you get clearer on what you need to say, via which method, and to which audience.

As you work on building out the specific tactics in your book marketing strategy, you can cross-reference the tactics you're coming up with and make notes of where your activity requires the creation of a piece of content, then come check your messages and methods list. More often than not, you will find you've got the perfect thing to say already identified, removing a brain barrier to getting on with reaching potential readers of your book.

9

Web Presence

Web presence can include a self-managed website that you own, a web page on your publishing partner's site, your LinkedIn or Facebook page, or even your Amazon author page. Your web presence can be one of the "methods" you can use to leverage your messages and build awareness of you and your books with your reader and influencer audiences.

Why You Need a Web Presence

You need a web presence because successful selling means being visible. Depending on your genre and your network, social media platforms alone might be sufficient. But this will rarely be the case. Many authors rely solely on the fact their book is on Amazon and consider that this is web presence enough. It isn't, at least not if you want to build your business through your book or build your author career.

One of the advantages to having a web presence is control: you can monitor traffic, engagement, interactions, and you can update and edit the content on the online property with relative ease. It also gives you an opportunity to drive profit back to a property that you own and that you have control of. You also have an opportunity – depending on what arrangement you have with your distributors, whether you're exclusive or wide – to sell directly from your website. This can give you greater control over revenue and expense.

If you choose to have a presence only on social media, or only on Amazon, for example, what's the one thing you're going to have to do if you want to promote your book? You're going to take out social media ads or pay for Amazon marketing services. You're going to give money to the Mark Zuckerbergs and Jeff Bezos's of the world. And those are people that already have enough money. They don't need yours.

You can use organic content from your social media pages to drive traffic to your own website. Even if you end up investing in some ads to boost that traffic, the end result is visitors to your own website, where they can engage in your business and buy your books directly. And you won't be sharing revenue or royalties with anyone else.

How to Decide

Determining which type of web presence is for you is all about your circumstances: how much time, money, and technical expertise you have access to. If you have lots of time, a bit of money, and some technical expertise, then you're probably okay to pull together a website on your own. There are some things you can do fairly simply. If you don't have any time and you don't have any technical expertise, but you have a bit of money, then you can hire professional help. And if you have zero of all three, then setting up a website or a webpage right now probably isn't the best thing.

You're the one who knows what works for you. If you do decide that you're going to build your own web presence, you're obviously going to want to pay attention to and consider search engine optimization (SEO). You'll also want to consider a free or inexpensive plug-in that helps you automate social posts that drive traffic back to the website. (My favourite is Nelio.) And you can also consider whether you want to embark on selling books direct from your website. Obviously, there are some logistics involved, and you also need to make sure that you have the right agreement with your distributors and that you're not exclusive.

But the main thing is to be sure, at a minimum, that your readers and potential readers can find you online. In an ideal world, you'll have full control over where you are online, so you remain firmly in control of your assets, your business, and your author career.

10

Author Photo

Your author photo is going to be a key element for your messages: most, if not all, of what you share as you promote your book will include, or should include, a professional author photo.

Many indie authors struggle with how to handle their author photo. They're shy, or modest, or frugal, and don't want to hire a professional photographer "just" for their author photo. If you haven't already got an awesome author photo displayed on the back cover of your book and/or in the About the Author section, now is the time to incorporate such a photo in your plans for marketing.

Why?

You're writing a book for people to read. Which means you have an audience of readers in mind. You want those readers to connect with your book. Whether it's your memoir, a self-help book, business book, professional development book, an award-worthy piece of journalistic nonfiction, or any one of the sub-genres of fiction, your readers are going to want to connect with you. Especially if they loved your book, they are going to gobble up the "About the Author" section at the back of the book. They might even Google you and see what else they can find out about you online.

A Reader-Author Connection

When I say "connect," I don't necessarily mean they'll pick up the phone. Although if they feel a connection when they look at your awesome author photo, they will be much more inclined to do that. I'm talking about a *feeling* of connection. Reading your words is one part of it. Seeing the eyes and face of the author whose words they have just spent eight or ten hours reading is another level altogether.

This acknowledgement that the reader wants to connect with you is a valuable two-way street. Do you want readers to look for and buy every other book you have written or will write? Do you want them to hire you for coaching or other services, or to purchase the suite of products you've written about after they read your book? If the answer is yes, then you definitely want to include a professional-quality author photo.

Let's dig a little further into the ramifications of the three main options: no photo, any photo, or a professional photo. And then we'll talk a little bit about how to get a great professional photo.

No Author Photo

In many cases, it's not horrible to forgo an author photo. *"Let readers focus on the words, rather than on the person who wrote them."* Well, sure. If you don't include an author photo you don't have to hire a professional photographer, you don't have to address the wrinkles or jowls or sharp nose or whatever else you hate about your own image (when did my hair turn from ginger to grey?).

You'll also remain an enigma to your reader. A disembodied

voice. Ask yourself this question: is it easier for you to trust someone when you can look them in the eyes? Without an author photo, you are missing out on a key way that you can build trust with your readers — who are leads and prospects for your author business.

A Non-Professional Photo

You might be tempted to use a favourite personal photo as your author photo. You look younger, or skinnier, or you really like the smile in this one photo.

You may have an emotional attachment to it, like the one Ingenium Books' US-based author Yvonne Caputo had with this photo of her sitting inside a B24 bomber, the same aircraft her father flew in WWII. Since that's also the subject of her book, an argument could be made that this is a great photo to use. In the case of this photo, there are three main problems: the dark background, the resolution, and the fact that without an explanatory caption, few will know she's sitting in a B24.

Non-professional, personal photos can be spotted a mile away for problems with resolution, composition, extraneous objects that detract the focus, and a whole host of other potential issues. All of which scream, "Amateur!" We may be indie authors, proud to self-publish, but we do not want to give anyone *any* reason to label our book as sub-par.

Professional Photo

As long as you hire a good photographer (as in, check references and look at the portfolio in advance!) you shouldn't be saddled with any of these amateur issues. Yes, you will have to pay for the service. You will also want to review licensing terms to be sure you can appropriately credit the photographer and legally use the photo in the way you intend. But you'll end up with a great-quality photo that will help imbue authenticity, credibility, and confidence around your book. That is what you want.

Direction for Your Photographer

Hiring a professional doesn't mean, for example, that you must resign yourself to a boring corporate-style suit-and-tie shot. Perhaps you want some personality and creativity to show through, or you want a photo that aligns with the theme of your book. You can help ensure you get the results you desire by a little preparation in advance.

1. Research and find examples of author photos that you like and dislike. Bring samples to the first meeting with the photographer.
2. Be sure you get a photo where readers can see your eyes. This is really important, especially for a business nonfiction book, when you want to build credibility and trust. If you write cloak-and-dagger mysteries this wouldn't be as important for obvious reasons.
3. Consider colour schemes and how the photo might fit with your cover design.
4. Request a series of poses or at least more than one. This is partly to give you more to choose from, but

also to give you flexibility and options: you might choose one pose for the back cover of your book, and another pose for your media kit or the poster you're making for your book launch event, and still another for your author webpage.
5. Think about the subject of your book and your area of expertise, and then think about scenes, settings, outfits, and props that might work to incorporate into the shoot. If you're a financial planner, you probably want at least a collar, if not a jacket and tie. But if you're a drummer, a T-shirt while sitting at your drum kit would be great.

Some Example Author Photos

Let's use some real-life author-photo examples and talk about why they work.

Henrik Mondrup

Henrik, from Denmark, needed a new author photo for his forthcoming book, *Achieving Change*. He had a perfectly good suit-and-tie headshot, but it was a few years old and didn't quite exude the level of calm, confidence, and competence we thought would be best for his book.

We can see Henrik's face and eyes. He has an open and relaxed body position, and he looks approachable and confident at the same time. This is a great author photo.

Yvonne Caputo

Once Yvonne realized her B24 navigator's seat photo wasn't going to be ideal as her author photo, she set out to hire a photographer and the results show. She's got two settings with

different colour schemes for a bit of flexibility.

Again, we can see Yvonne's face and eyes, her body language is relaxed and comfortable, and she looks approachable and open. This also has the advantage of having a colour scheme that blends well with the cover design of her forthcoming book, *Flying With Dad*.

Lauren Clucas

As a South African relationship counsellor whose book, <u>Wanted</u>, is about relationships, Lauren opted for closer framing that really lets you connect with her eyes and face. Establishing trust is key for Lauren, at a more intimate level than is necessary for Yvonne's memoir or Henrik's book about creating digital learning courses.

So before you decide whether to skip including an author photo, and before you make a mistake on which photo to use, think through your original objectives for you and your book. You'll soon find that it will be clear which option will help you achieve your goals and objectives. My bias is that we indie authors should put our best foot forward and stand up tall, claiming our book by including the best possible author photo.

Social Media

Social media is a big deal for authors. I like to call social media YOS: Your Own Stuff, meaning your online profiles and platforms. This includes LinkedIn, Twitter, Instagram, Facebook, Amazon, Amazon Author Central, and Pinterest. You'll see some of these platforms might overlap with your overall web presence.

Why Do You Want to Be on Social Media?

Your social media footprint is a foundational element in your marketing toolkit. It is instrumental in helping you build author, book, speaking, and brand awareness. And it's also going to play key roles in helping you with speaking engagements and book sales objectives.

How to Determine the Right Social Media Approach

How do you figure out the right social media approach for you and what do you include about this in your book marketing strategy?

You want to find out *where* your readers and your influencers are on social media. Are they on LinkedIn but not Pinterest? Or do they rock the Twitter-verse? It might be that different segments of your audiences are on different platforms. You want to be where they are.

To find out where your readers are, you'll take the results of your work on your target audience, from chapter 3, *Your Target Audience*, and then research the demographics of each of the social platforms. To do this, start by entering into your favourite search engine the phrase, "demographics of users of [insert social platform name]".

Then you'll match up the results of what you've found for the demographics of the social media platform with who your target audience is.

Setting Up Profiles and Claiming Handles

Once you know where your readers are on social media, you'll want to set up your own social profiles and claim your social media handles. The social media handle is essentially a text code that lets people find you. So, for example, on Twitter, Ingenium Books' handle is @ingeniumbooks. Every Twitter handle starts with the @ symbol and then whatever name you choose. Facebook is the same. If you set up an author page on Facebook, the handle is the name that you give it when you set up the page and the account. Research your chosen handle first to be sure it isn't already in use. You don't want to confuse your readers, or worse, send them to the wrong account.

Set up accounts and claim social media handles even on platforms where you're not yet active, even if you don't think you'll want to be on that particular platform. If you decide a year from now that you *do* want to be on the platform, your desired handle will still be available for you because you've reserved it. Otherwise, someone else might have snatched it up.

To find you, people type in the handle into a webpage or as a

URL and it will bring up your Facebook page or your Twitter account. They can now use it to tag you in conversations.

Your handle can be the name of your book, or the series, or your business, or your author name. If your book is about or related to your business, it might make sense to choose a handle related to your business. If you've written a memoir or self-help book and you think you might be writing more books, it probably makes more sense to choose your author name as the handle. This way you only need to keep track of one account on the relevant social media platform.

Claiming your social media handles doesn't mean that you have to start being active right away. It just means you own the property and it is in your control. Then, should you decide to start, you already have something where the branding aligns with the book and with you as author.

Connecting With Your Audiences

In the social media section of your strategy, you want to articulate how you're going to connect with your audience and your influencers in the media, who they are, where they are, and obviously increase brand awareness. It's important to remember the 80/20 rule: 80 percent of your social media activity should be helpful and engaging and only 20 percent should be promotional.

12

Public Relations (PR)

PR is *earned media* as opposed to *paid media*. Paid media is an ad or placement that you pay for. Instead, with earned media, you're enlisting the interest of a reporter to write about you. I also call this OPS, or Other People's Stuff. You'll remember that I call social media YOS, Your Own Stuff. So, in essence, PR involves getting printed in OPS, Other People's Stuff. It's traditional media, radio, TV, print, and online media like *Huffington Post*. It's even getting in front of influencers: folks who have popular or high-profile blogs or social media accounts with lots of followers.

Why Consider PR

PR is one of the most effective and economical methods in book promotion because of the reach and the inferred credibility from media coverage. Think about the last time you saw or read or listened to an interview with an author. It doesn't matter whether they're good or new or well established; if you've heard an interview with them you automatically think, "Oh, they must be good because so-and-so's doing an interview." That's what you want with your own author career and with your own book.

How to Plan Your PR

There are eight steps to planning your PR, and I'll explain the details of each in a moment. First, here's the order:

Step 1. Plan your focus
Step 2. Compile a media list
Step 3. Decide on your distribution method
Step 4. Engage a professional to write your media release
Step 5. Contact the most influential media on your list
Step 6. Contact the next level of influential media on your list
Step 7. Wait the promised period of time
Step 8. Launch your paid distribution

Step 1. Plan Your Focus

If you're going to embark on a public relations initiative, you need to come up with something edgy enough to attract media attention. You need to assess and then boost the newsworthiness of your message.

PR is not, "Hey Mom, look what I've done." It is about what's new, what's ground-breaking, what's different. Is there a new, local, or regional angle on a story that is prominent in the media right now? Are you shining new light on a subject of broad interest? Can you contribute something unique to a conversation that's already happening in the media? You need to say something that's different, new, or newsworthy. The fact that you've spent years working on the book and have finally published is not, sadly, newsworthy.

Remember your USP? This is really important for PR. Use your USP as you plan your focus and as you write your emails and media releases.

Step 2. Compile a Media List

Compile a list of media contacts that you'll reach out to directly. Start with anyone you might know who is in the media, then move to those with the highest profile, the biggest names, and with the most influence. Research the stories they've published in the last few months: you don't want to pitch to a reporter who just wrote about something similar last week. They won't be interested. Also research which reporters and media outlets have published stories on the general subject area you'll be asking them to write about. If you write leadership handbooks, it won't make sense to pitch to reporters or outlets that cover medical news, unless your book is for leaders in the medical field.

Organize your list into sections: the most influential at the top and the least influential at the end. This is so the first people you contact will yield the best results if they do indeed pick up your story.

I recommend a combination of personal outreach and paid distribution.

Step 3. Decide on Your Paid Distribution Method

Paid distribution is paying to push your media release out through wire services, which are news agencies that supply syndicated and other news by 'wire' to television and radio stations, newspapers, and certain online media properties. There it will be seen by the reporters and assignment editors deciding what stories are going to be written that day.

Some paid distribution services only disseminate your release to online properties, like Yahoo News and other aggregators, and not to the bigger media outlets like the New York Times or Guardian or Globe and Mail. These packages tend to be cheaper. They are also less effective for getting an actual reporter interested in writing about you, your book, or your business, unless you're a big star or your pitch is particularly newsworthy.

Media release distribution services include PR Newswire and PR Web in the US, Canada Newswire and Canadian Press in Canada, PR Wire and Get the Word Out in Australia, PressAt and PRMax in the UK. I'm not endorsing any of these, and there are many more. Just do a search for "media release distribution services + [your jurisdiction]" to find additional options. There are similar services that can help you distribute to bloggers. Search for "blogger outreach + [your jurisdiction]."

Fees vary for each distribution service, depending how broad or specific you want the distribution, e.g. just to your local area or nation-wide. The fee is also often contingent on word count, inclusion of images, a logo, and optional social media add-ons.

If you keep your media release to somewhere between 250 and 500 words, including headlines and the datelines, and don't include any images, for example, you could spend up to a few hundred dollars. If you want a longer release, and you want it branded (e.g. with your logo or image of your book cover), and you choose to add a social media distribution component, you could spend in the neighbourhood of $1000USD.

Step 4. Engage a Professional to Write Your Media Release

Media releases require effective headlines, subheadings, a location and dateline, and a great lead paragraph. They need to be structured into the news-style pyramid, which is the formula journalists use to ensure that any reader can get the gist of the story whether they stop reading after the headline, after the first paragraph, or any other paragraph after that. In other words, people do not have to read the entire release to understand the story.

There are other tricks that a pro will help you tease out in a media release, too. Inclusion of quotes that can be lifted verbatim, links to supporting research or stories, and relevant and interesting quick facts at the end.

Writing a media release is a particular style of writing — in the same way the copywriting for the back cover of your book or your Amazon sales page requires a different and specific skillset from the one you employ when writing your manuscript.

If you are going to choose PR, it will be worth it to hire someone skilled in the art of writing a good media release. You can even have them tailor a media release for a particular publication or media outlet.

Step 5. Contact the Most Influential Media on Your List from Item Number Two

Conduct your personal media outreach before you do any paid distribution. Reporters always want to think they've got the scoop, or an exclusive, meaning they have the story first.

Personal outreach to a specific reporter can lead to a major media story written about you and your book, however it is the most difficult result to achieve. You need an excellent and newsworthy hook and professionally-crafted content that will contribute to a broader societal, economic, or social issue.

When reaching out to the people on your media list, remember that they get dozens, if not hundreds, of such solicitations every week. And remember that the timing of any publication is beyond your control, often beyond the reporter's control too. Reporters and the stories they cover are heavily influenced by what ELSE is happening in the world. You may connect with a reporter who plans to write a story, but then something big happens. In the movie *Spotlight*, about the investigative team of reporters at the Boston Globe who first broke the story of the systematic sexual abuse of children by Catholic priests, the team had been investigating for more than a year and were about to publish. Then 9/11 happened and those investigative reporters were assigned 9/11-related stories. Was the child sex abuse story important? Yes. It still got published, but it was delayed by a few months. It's not personal when this happens, it's news.

Back to contacting the reporters. Consider reaching out by phone and email. Keep your introductory message short and to the point. Do not include the full media release until they say they are interested. Do make reference to other stories they have done that make you think they might be interested in yours. Your message might go something like this:

> "Hello, I'd like to offer you an exclusive on a story about [insert your headline from the media release]. I see you've recently covered stories on [insert the related story/stories they've done] and I thought this would be a good fit. I'm going to be issuing a release in the next [few days/week] and I wanted to give you first access. I'm the author of the book [insert title] and I look forward to hearing back from you."

Step 6. Contact the Next Level of Influential Media on Your List

Repeat the process from step number five with the contacts on the next level on your list.

Step 7. Wait the Allotted Time

After steps five and six, you'll wait the allotted period of time before you take the next steps.

Step 8. Launch Your Paid Distribution

When you've completed all the personal outreach to your list, and/or when someone has published your story, then you can move to launch your paid distribution.

You'll be asked to choose your release date and time, confirm your geographic and sector distribution, and you'll be set to go.

A note about the "media contact" section at the bottom of your media release; be sure you have a person listed who can actually be reached at the phone number and email you provide. Be sure they are able to respond and get any additional information the journalist asks for *fast*.

Not many reporters these days have the luxury of long lead times for their stories. If they're interested, you may have caught them with a hole to fill in an hour, or later today. Don't blow this opportunity by failing to properly set up the expectations for your media contact to respond.

I remember when I was a journalist, my dad complained about a "pushy" reporter he had dealt with in his role at work. He called me afterward and said, "You're not pushy like that, are you?" I had to tell him that his daughter was indeed "pushy" when she needed to be and she was looking for someone to interview, or to provide or confirm facts and context for stories. I'm not otherwise a pushy person. But I had a deadline and my responsibility was to publish the story whether or not all my inquiries received responses. These reporters that you want to deal with are the same. Be sure you and whoever you have listed on the bottom of your release is ready to respond. Twenty-four hours is too long.

A final word about public relations: your campaign should be ongoing, even long after you've published your book. Keep abreast of the latest news and other developments related to the subject matter of your book. Things change all the time and what may not have been a hook before can suddenly become one now.

Media Kit

PR is about proactive outreach and it's about responding when a reporter or blogger expresses interest. Having a thorough and well-planned media kit is key to being and looking professional and organized.

A note about terminology: I like to say *media kit* and *media release* instead of *press kit* and *press release*. They are technically the same thing, but *press release* is an outdated term from the days when news was delivered via the printing press. It doesn't reflect the evolution of news dissemination via broadcast (television and radio) or online.

You'll want to have your media kit with you at your book launch and any book signing events. As a marketing opportunity, your book-signing event will be more effective if it does get some media coverage. Media coverage creates visibility: more people will recognize your name and the title of your book. Media coverage also breeds more media coverage: a story in a local newspaper may lead to a television interview, for instance. (I know this because, as a television reporter back in the day, one great way to come up with my daily story was to scour the local, regional, and weekly papers to find little nuggets I might be able to expand on or explore from a new perspective.)

Book signings tend to be busy events and you won't have time for in-depth interviews with journalists or book bloggers. That's why you need a media kit that you can provide at the event. This way, they get all the basic information about you and your book. They then simply need to follow up with you if they have any more questions.

Here's what to include in your media kit:

- A book summary page: This page should include the book title, your name, the name of the publisher, the ISBNs for every format of the book, the page count,

the retail price for every format, the book cover image and information about where to buy the book.
- An author biography: This should be a short description of who you are. Include a good quality photograph of yourself, too.
- A list of book reviews and testimonials: You may include short quotes to pique the media's interest. Then, add links to the full reviews and testimonials too.
- A list of the media coverage you've already received: Include details of the type of coverage – newspaper articles, radio interviews, and the like – with links to any coverage that has appeared online.
- A media release: Your media release should be a general release with information about the book. Also include a bit about you and why you wrote the book.
- Contact information: Try to have at least a link to your website on every page in your media kit, and a separate page with more detailed contact information too: your phone number, email address, website and social media information. If you have a publisher, include their contact details too.

Package and Plan for the Media

Put together all the information in a neat folder or large envelope. Also include a USB stick with digital copies of everything, including both hi-res and web-friendly images of you and your book cover.

About two or three weeks before every event, including book signings, speeches, workshops, and library talks, consider inviting journalists and book bloggers. Focus on those in the local area but don't forget to invite the regional and national media too. Coordinate with the venue to find out who they've invited and make a list of everyone who has confirmed that they will attend. This will help you determine how many media kits to prepare. Bring a few extras, just in case.

Make your media kit available in downloadable formats on your website in an area for media. Nothing looks as impressive as an author or business owner who is so well prepared as to have an advance media kit ready and available. Even if you haven't had a lot of media coverage, it will look as though you have.

13

Reader Reviews

Reader reviews are the all-important social proof that others use to make their book-buying decisions. It's the reviews that are on Amazon, Kindle, Kobo, Goodreads, your website, the local paper, and so on. And it also includes advance-copy reader reviews, which are the reviews you obtain from providing pre-published copies of the book for free to readers who may decide to post a review.

Why Focus on Reviews

Here are seven reasons reader reviews are important.

1. THEY TELL POTENTIAL READERS WHAT TO EXPECT

The most obvious advantage of reader reviews is that they can tell us what the book is about, what the writing is like, even what emotions the book conjures up. If your book gets good reviews from people who have read it, others may want to read it too.

. . .

2. Reader Reviews Improve Visibility

The more reviews your book has on Amazon, the more likely it is that it will pop up as a suggested product when someone is trying to navigate the thousands of books available on the website. Many positive reviews can also result in a higher ranking. This in turn increases the chances of people actually buying your book. After all, very few people scroll beyond the first or second page of listed books before making a purchase.

3. Reader Reviews Can Get You Promotional Deals

E-book retailers often have promotions such as Amazon's Kindle Monthly Deals, where your book enjoys greater visibility on the site for a specific period of time. Books with more reviews usually get picked more readily than those with only a handful of reviews. So, lots of positive reviews can score you that coveted spot on the promotions list. These promotions often go hand in hand with a reduced selling price for the duration of the promotion. A lower selling price for a short period can be a good thing: it may encourage more people to buy your book, and more reviews, which then lead to more sales, even once the promotion is over and your book is selling at its regular price again.

4. Reader Reviews Can Help You Get into BookBub

BookBub can be an author's best marketing friend. This free but highly competitive service provides subscribers with promotional deals, recommendations, and author updates. Unlike sites like Amazon, BookBub doesn't sell books but simply tells its subscribers about the books that are available on retail sites like Amazon, Nook and Apple Books. However, BookBub doesn't recommend just any book. In fact, the vast majority of books submitted to BookBub are rejected. With lots of good reader reviews, your book stands a higher chance of being accepted. And once you have BookBub's support, the sky's the limit.

5. READER REVIEWS CAN HELP YOU GET YOUR BOOK INTO BOOKSTORES.

Reviews help provide evidence to book store operators that there is an eager audience for your book — which means a business opportunity for them. Indie bookstores provide a more personal book-buying experience than the big-name chains. Generally, bibliophiles love their local bookstore: the one where the employees know their name, their reading preferences, and can give them personalized recommendations. Good reviews on a site like Goodreads can help you to convince those indie bookstores to stock your book. They can also help convince the store's employees to read your book and make it their "staff pick," which will lead to more sales.

6. READER REVIEWS CAN LEAD TO BIGGER THINGS

When readers love your book — and say so on a public platform like a review site — this can help your book get noticed by those oh-so-important players in the industry. As a new indie author, your chances of getting reviewed by a publication like the New York Times Book Review or Publishers Weekly are close to none. Get lots of great reader reviews on Goodreads or Amazon, though, and it just might pique the interest of these renowned publications.

It's not only the professional reviewers who might notice your book, though. Traditional publishers may notice all those five-star reviews on Goodreads and decide that you're the next big thing. Next, you'll want to be sure you're informed about selling your rights, but that's for another day.

· · ·

7. Reader Reviews Can Help You Improve

While all of the reasons we've discussed so far boil down to positive reader reviews leading to more sales, negative reader reviews can be important sources of feedback. They're tough, of course. However, if they point to plot or structure problems, or — heaven forbid — typos and other errors, this is valuable feedback you can heed to make your next book better. You can use this feedback to help you improve. You can have your book proofread again for the next edition, for instance. Or you can work on your writing skills. The key is to listen to what your reviewers say without collapsing into a heap of self-doubt.

How to Solicit Reader Reviews

Reader reviews rarely happen by osmosis. There are some authors who just seem to attract reader reviews: all they have to do is pop a book up on their sales platform of choice and reviews roll in. That's not the norm. Most of us have to work at it. And it means planning your advance reader review strategy pre-launch, so that you can have a number of folks who have read your book before it gets published. When your book goes live, they are encouraged to leave their reviews. A note here, Amazon's rules (at the time of this writing) mean you cannot offer a free copy of your book *in exchange* for a review. You will want to encourage your advance review copy readers to declare, "I received a free advance copy of this book," in any honest review they do post.

You may not wish to engage in an advance review copy strategy at all: there is a school of thought that this is not ethical, despite being a common tactic employed by traditional publishers. You decide.

In any case you want to plan your post-publishing reader review strategy. Consider including the following:

1. Posting a notice encouraging reviews in the front and

back matter of your book, so that when readers are most ready to review (as soon as they've finished reading the book) they will be reminded about how important it is to an author and that you'll be very grateful.
2. Publish a blog post or article on your site explaining why reader reviews are so important today and include links to where readers of your book(s) can post those reviews.
3. Look for promotion opportunities, where your book gets included, for example, in someone else's email blast. There are a number of these services out there, at a range of fees. I've found one on Fiverr, where for $5 or $10 they'd include a book in a couple of email blasts, and I did notice an uptick in sales and views. The field is changing all the time, so a quick online search for "book promotion services for authors" should get you an interesting field of options.
4. Reach out to reviewers directly via email, politely and briefly making the request, including a very concise summary of your book, where they can find it (e.g. Amazon) and finally a little about you. Do not chase them — if you get a review from them, great. If you don't, don't make a nuisance of yourself by continuing to follow up.

14

Email Marketing

Email marketing is a system where you offer something of value, for free, in exchange for an email address. You nurture and cultivate this growing list of interested readers through a series of emails that are designed to inform, assist, and then of course, sell your books or business services.

Why Email Marketing?

Email marketing works. It is a proven approach to help build a network of fans: readers, book buyers, and even past and future clients.

How to Plan Your Email Marketing Strategy

There's more to embarking on email marketing than can be covered in this book. The point is to consider email marketing in your book marketing mix and plan to incorporate the steps in your book marketing strategy. There are entire courses dedicated to this. Nick Stephenson's *Your First 10k Readers* is one example. There are others, and it involves writing the right kind of content in your "nurturing sequence" emails and leading members of your list along a predetermined "funnel" to a point where they are ready to buy books from you.

With an email marketing strategy, you need one or more "lead magnets," which are free giveaways that people want enough that they'll give you their name and email address in exchange for access. This might be a free chapter of your book, or an opinion piece, a how-to document or infographic.

Then you will need an email marketing system like Mailchimp, MailerLite, ConvertKit, or Constant Contact. You'll need to become familiar with privacy rules and laws like GDPR, which is the European Union's General Data Protection Regulation, that aim to ensure that people remain in control of their personal information. You'll need to include a relevant privacy notice on your website and then adhere to those rules, which include not emailing anyone for purposes other than what they agreed to when they gave you their email, and not sharing any contact information with anyone outside your organization for any purpose not already declared.

Your marketing strategy objectives are going to guide you in terms of how deep you need to get into email marketing and how much email automation you need. So, refer back to your objectives. That will help guide you with how much time and effort you need to put into email marketing.

15

Promotional Products

Promotional products are the materials that promote you and your book. I'm talking about things like bookmarks, business cards, postcards, and your book package (a document that contains the book's title, cover, description, table of contents, author bio, keywords and sales categories). They may be physical or electronic and you may hand them out in person, via email, or on social media or your website.

This is different from promotional content, which are the messages we discussed in chapter 8, *Messages & Methods*. Promotional products are some of the methods you'll use to deliver those messages. Promotional products are about branding: using them is about leaving something in someone's hands so they remember you.

Why Incorporate Promotional Products

Imagine you've gone to a meeting and you've been introduced to someone new.

"Hi! What do you do?" they ask.

"I'm an author and I've just released a new book."

"Oh, that's fantastic," they say. "What book is it?"

You whip out one of your promotional products, whether it's a business card or a bookmark or a postcard or whatever, and you give it to them. They go home and three, four, or eight hours later they empty their pockets or their purse and out comes your promotional product. "Oh yeah," they say to themselves. And they take it over to the computer and they buy your book.

How to Plan Your Promo Products

When you're thinking about what promotional products might work for you, take a look at everything else you've done so far in the strategy, where you're planning to go out and meet people and talk to them about your book, and what's going to make sense in that context. A common promotional product for authors is a bookmark. Postcards are less common, but because they're a different size and little bit unusual, they might help you stand out.

Promo products can also be a collection of other products, like a speaker's kit, which you could adapt from or double as your media kit from chapter 11, *Public Relations*. If you want somebody to hire you to speak at their conference, you need to make sure that you have something nice looking and professional to hand out. If you want to get your book into local or independent bookstores, you can walk in and personally provide your manager with a single-page, two-sided glossy book package. Promo products also include your media kit and definitely professional author photos.

Don't discount your voice as a promotional product either. For example, you're out talking about your book with somebody – family and friends, or your next-door neighbour, or you're in a restaurant. If you get the word out to one person, that person speaks with another person or two other people. Those two people speak with another two or four others. The word spreads. So, don't discount speaking often and all the time about who you are as an author and what your book is about, remembering to include what problem your book solves for the reader.

When you're having a conversation with someone and you can also hand them something tangible, they'll remember you and your book.

"Flying With Dad"
business card front

For example, we prepared a business card for Yvonne Caputo to take on her 2018 visit to England and the airbase where her father was stationed in World War II.

Even though the book wasn't coming out until 2019, Yvonne personally introduced herself to bookstore owners. She spoke to museum chairpersons and historical societies. And almost a year before her book came out, we were receiving calls and emails from people asking us to put their names on our list and let them know when her book is released.

That speaks to the power of the promotional products that you can create. And you don't have to wait until your book is published for them to bear fruit.

People are inundated with stuff though, so you want to make sure your promotional products are authentic, attractive and high quality.

"Flying With Dad"
business card back

16

Your Book Launch

Your book launch comprises the actual act of making your book available for sale and any book launch event or events you decide to hold. You get to decide the order: hold a launch event when your book is in pre-sale mode and then publish; or publish and even a week or a month or months later hold one or more book launch events.

Why Strategize Your Book Launch?

There is a sense of relief that comes with finally launching your book. All the hard work is done and now you can just sit and wait for the money to come rolling in, right? Not so fast.

Many authors just want to get it "out there" and when everything is ready, they can't resist the temptation to simply publish all formats of the book at the same time. I know, I did this with my first book, *Rock Your Business: 26 Essential Lessons to Start, Run, and Grow Your New Business from the Ground Up*, co-written with my husband and business partner John Wagner-Stafford. If, after you've read the rest of this chapter, you still think this is best for you, no problem. Think it through first.

For indie authors, the book launch is less a single event and more a state of mind. Think long and sustaining rather than short and intense. The opportunity to stagger your book launch by format feeds into this notion.

Instead of launching the hardback, paperback, e-book and audio formats of your book all at the same time, consider the marketing impact of launching them one at a time, with a few weeks or months in between.

You might make your e-book available for pre-order first. Amazon KDP gives you up to ninety days to publish after that. During this time you can be promoting your book, for example, on your own website and social platforms and by writing guest posts for others. You can be continuing to secure endorsements and editorial reviews.

Within ninety days, you publish the e-book. Then you wait thirty, sixty, or however many days before publishing the paperback version, and then another six months to a year before you publish hardback and audiobook.

You could also begin with the launch of a hardback, although this won't work for a KDP pre-order scenario. Launching hardback or hardcover first is a common tactic in the traditional publishing world, with paperback and e-book formats often coming out as much as a year later.

"That sounds like a lot of extra work," you might say. It is. You'll need a more comprehensive plan and some extra project management. But there are several advantages of staggering your book launches by format.

1. Extra Marketing Opportunities

The first—and main—advantage is the extra marketing opportunities a strategy like this creates. With every product launch, you can create more buzz with marketing activities like social media posts, interviews, advertising, and speaking engagements. You get more people talking about and interested in buying your book. This keeps the momentum going and your sales consistent or growing, bringing the money in over a longer term. Launching everything at once, in contrast, can mean lots of sales in the first days or weeks and then ... nothing, as your potential readers have moved on to the next big thing.

Amazon's sales ranking is based on historic and recent sales activity, but it weights recent activity more heavily. A burst of sales around launch with a drop later will harm your sales rank, so staggering the release by format is a strategy that helps you maintain consistent or growing sales.

2. The Chance to Revise Your Marketing Strategy

Staggering the launch by format gives you the chance to revise your marketing approach if you need to.

With each format launch, you can check how well that product is received. You can also see who is buying – and who isn't. This means you can rethink how to target those readers who haven't been convinced yet that they should buy your book. For example, let's say that you find that it's mostly older professional males, aged forty-five to sixty-five who buy the hardback version of your book, but you would really like the female professionals between thirty-five and fifty to read your book too. So, with staggered launches, you have more time to adjust your marketing activities so that you can target different segments of your audience for the paperback e-book and audio-book formats.

3. The Chance to Make Changes

In the tech industry, staggered product launches give developers the opportunity to identify and fix glitches in programs or games. This is another reason to consider staggering the launches of your book formats: it allows you to make changes. For example, after the launch of the hardback book, you may get a respected expert in the field to write a new foreword, which you can then include in the paperback or e-book to give your book extra credibility. You can also fix problems with the content, from typos to factual errors. Or you can add illustrations. And of course, in this rapidly changing world, new information may come to light that you can include in the later versions of your book.

These book launch events don't have to be restricted to only the first launch: another advantage of a staggered format launch is that you can plan to hold launch events tailored to different audiences to coincide with the publication of each format. For your hardcover, hold an event at a downtown location and invite professionals and an older crowd more likely to appreciate a hardcover. Hold another event when the paperback and e-book come out and choose a venue that's a little hipper to attract the younger members of your reader audience. You get the picture.

The point is that you could plan a book signing event every month or two. Include it in the strategy to ensure you have regular book marketing activities planned. You get back only what you put in.

Book Signing Kit

Book-signing events can be a valuable piece of your marketing pie. Like everything else related to being an author, you can't just waltz into a book-signing event, carrying only your pen and a few extra copies of your baby (that's your book), and expect it to go well. It's all about making it easy for you to hold these events, to have everything on hand that you need to bring, and to take care of as much as possible in advance so nothing gets in your way of rocking your book signing events.

So, here's what you need in your book-signing kit.

1. Pens

Sounds too simple, doesn't it? Don't assume that the venue will provide pens for your book-signing event. Bring your own, with several back-ups. Test the pens beforehand to make sure that they work. You may also want to consider choosing pens that are comfortable to use: your hand will get tired from all that writing. (Think positive!)

2. An Assistant

Trying to handle every aspect of your book signing on your own can be very stressful. Sometimes impossible. This is especially true if you also have to handle the book sales at the event. Bring an assistant who can do the running around, bring you something to drink, and handle the sales, so you can focus on connecting with your readers.

3. Business Cards and Other Promotional Products

Here's where the items you started thinking about in chapter 14, *Promotional Products*, come in handy. Load your book-signing kit with business cards, bookmarks or postcards. You can hand these to people who might want you to speak at one of their events, or to give to friends and colleagues they think would benefit from reading (and buying) your book.

4. A Notebook

You will meet people who are valuable contacts for future engagements. When you hand them your business card, take down their contact details too so you can follow up with them. This could be the notes function in your smartphone or tablet, but you want to make sure you can jot notes quickly without losing eye contact with the speaker for too long or getting distracted by a bunch of other message alerts.

5. Backup (Extra) Books

Deciding how many books to buy and bring to your book signing is more art than science. It's unlikely that you'll sell 500 at a single signing event, but if you've organized and promoted the event and your location is conducive to extra traffic, you'll likely sell more than five. If you have a series of signing events lined up in a heavy book-buying period, say pre-Christmas, it might be safe to have 250 copies printed and understand that you might be left with a few dozen and that will be a success.

6. Post-It Notes

Zach, Zack and Zac will be very disappointed if you get the spelling of their name wrong. You can ask an assistant to let your readers write their names on a post-it or sticky note and attach it to their copy of your book. This way, you only need to refer to the post-it instead of having to go through the endless ritual of, "How do you spell that?"

7. A Cash Box and Receipts

Depending on the location of your book-signing event and the arrangement you have with the bookstore manager, you will likely have to handle the book sales yourself. Bring a cashbox containing at least twice the change you think you'll need. Also bring a receipt book.

8. Your Best Selfie-Ready Face

Your readers will really appreciate it if you're willing to let them take selfies with you. If you're lucky, these pictures will end up on their social media profiles, so you want to look presentable. At least make sure you don't have spinach stuck in your teeth. You'll also want to be sure your assistant takes plenty of photos and video, if possible, during the event. These can be shared via social media during and after the event, and make great promotional images when you're spreading the word about your next book-signing event.

9. Prepared Remarks

You may wish to kick off the book signing event with a few remarks, depending on whether you've invited family, friends and colleagues to a launch event, or you're being given space in a bookstore and you're trying to attract foot traffic to your table. In the case of the former, prepare an engaging talk that will charm your audience. Include a short excerpt from the book and include that. Keep it short, though: you want to have enough time to sign everyone's copy of your book.

10. Book Package

This is the document we discussed in chapter 14, *Promotional Products*, that contains the book's title, cover, sales description, table of contents, author bio, keywords and sales categories.

Outstanding Book-Signing Kit = Better Results

The time and effort you put into assembling a book-signing kit will be well spent. The venue, your readers, your assistant, and the press will be impressed. Expect more interviews, more coverage, more invitations to speak at other events, and more sales. It will help you achieve better results overall.

Advertising

Advertising means paying someone else to help you promote your message. You can pay Internet giants like Amazon, Facebook, Twitter, LinkedIn, Google Ads and a host of other platforms and companies to run or display ads about you and your book.

Why Advertise

Sometimes you just need a little boost. And sometimes the cards are stacked against you, especially in what's called the 'pay to play' environment of Amazon and Facebook. On those two platforms your organic messages, posts, and book listing are not treated with priority, meaning far fewer people will be shown information about your book.

How to Plan Advertising

The first consideration is whether you have a budget to invest in some ads. If you do, great. With that budget in mind, you'll need to sort out which platform is going to make the most sense for where your readers are, for the objectives you have set, and for the subject and genre of your book.

Something to consider here is weighing the value of having your book available for sale on your own website and driving traffic through paid Google Ads. You must not have agreed to an exclusive arrangement with Amazon or any other seller, and this helps you avoid putting all your eggs in one basket. You'll pay Google to promote an ad that drives traffic to your website, but then you keep a far greater percentage of the resulting book sales because you're not sharing royalties with distributors like Amazon or Kobo or Apple iBooks.

Most authors, especially those just starting out, or those who really only plan to publish one book about their business, for example, are happy to let the big boys sell their book and not worry about having to ship and invoice and all that goes along with selling your book on your own site.

Choosing Where to Advertise

One of the challenges with including advertising in your book marketing strategy is that it is almost always a complex endeavour. You can hire people with expertise in advertising on one platform or the other, and while this might work for some, there's the twin drawbacks of the extra cost and the fact you aren't learning for next time.

Doing it yourself means a steep learning curve, particularly with Facebook advertising, Amazon Marketing Services, and Google Ads. There are long and detailed courses you can take, via sites like Udemy and elsewhere, where the price tag might be reasonable, but the hours required to complete the course and learn what you need to know is like learning a new language. I recently signed up for a Google Ads course on Udemy, thrilled to pay just $20 for the course, and four weeks later I was still only a third of the way through the course. Between running a business, working with clients on their books, and writing my own books, I could only commit two to three hours per week to the course.

Here is a high-level look at some of the benefits and drawbacks with advertising on the major platforms.

AMAZON MARKETING SERVICES (AMS)

AMS makes a lot of sense given that your ad on Amazon will be shown to people who are looking for books just like yours. *"Books about buying baby clothes,"* for example, could be a search term entered by someone desperate to find your new book with everything the new mom needs to know about outfitting her newborn. She's looking, you're offering, it's a match made in heaven. You can launch an ad, or a series of ads, from within your Amazon KDP dashboard. From there it gets progressively more complex. Categories, keywords, bids, oh my. Not a bad idea to take a course or read one of the books available that explain how to launch, monitor, and profit with the help of AMS.

GOOGLE ADS

I love the idea of Google Ads because, similar to Amazon advertising, your ads are shown to people who are explicitly searching for your search terms. Even though Google Ads are one step removed from Amazon, they might make more sense if you're planning to sell your book directly from your own website.

FACEBOOK

Facebook will present your ad to an audience of your choosing, and then selectively display that ad to those most likely to be interested in what you're selling. It's a great way to raise awareness and build your author brand. The challenge with

Facebook ads is that you're advertising to people *who aren't necessarily in the market to buy a book*. Still, with clever copywriting, great imagery, and a little know-how in the back end of Facebook Business Manager you can drive some new traffic to your FB author page, or your website, or even your book's page on Amazon.

There are many other advertising opportunities. You can spend as little as $5 to get into someone else's single email blast and you can spend more than you'd ever intended on advertising if you're not careful. Be prepared, do your research, and match your advertising activities with your objectives and your budget.

PART III. TAKING ACTION

Tactical Timeline

The tactical timeline is one of the magical pieces of the marketing strategy. (Ok, I'm a nerd.) It includes all your planned activities plotted on a timeline or calendar, so you know what you need to do and when. It's where the rubber hits the road.

Why Create a Tactical Timeline?

Creating a tactical timeline will allow you to create space in your brain so you'll be ready to take action. It lets you see when you might be overloaded and what you might be able to shift when you need to create some space. If you're like me, I sometimes wake up in the morning with a sense of overwhelm because the to-do list in my head is long. I can't decide what to focus on that morning or that day. On those days, more numerous than I care to admit, all you and I have to do is open up the tactical timeline, look at the book marketing tasks you'd planned for this week and for today. Boom. You've got your focus. This tool gives you power in decision making and a sense of control.

Here's a sample of what one of our tactical timelines looks like.

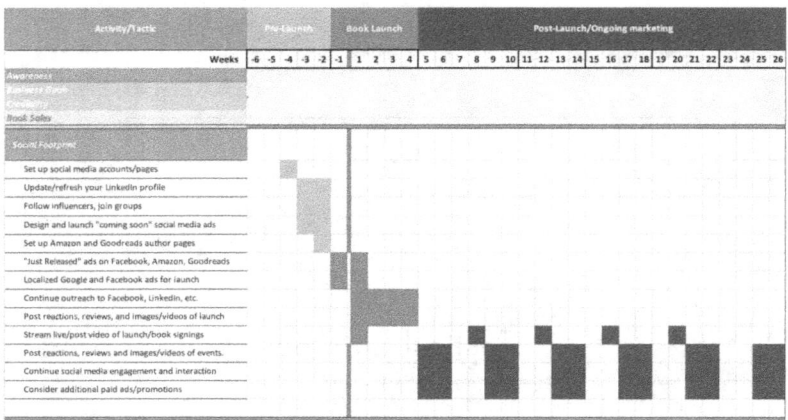

How to Create Your Own Tactical Timeline?

This part can be fun. Or maybe not. It depends on whether you like working with spreadsheets. I like looking at them but building them isn't my favourite thing. I'm lucky that my husband and business partner at Ingenium Books, John, is a whiz. So "we" use Excel to draw up the tactical timelines that accompany our book marketing strategies. We've tried other tools, including different types of online software, and we keep coming back to Excel. It simply works. It's easy. It's fast.

In our example image of a tactical timeline, you'll see the left-hand column is where we list each activity or task. At the top of that column you will see shaded rows. You're seeing this is shades of grey but our original has red for the category of building awareness, blue for the category of business goals, green for credibility, and yellow for book sales. These correspond to the objectives that the author in our sample timeline wanted to achieve for her book. You can choose your own colours and your own categories. You will then pull together the list of tactics and organize them into groups based on which objective they help you reach, so you always know at a glance which tactic is associated with which goal.

Along the top, moving toward the right, you'll see columns for pre-launch, book launch, then post-launch and ongoing marketing. We used to put actual dates in these columns, e.g. we'd say February first for the start of the pre-launch period, March first for the book launch, and April first for the post-launch period. Well, we discovered that the dates kept shifting and we kept having to edit our tactical timelines. Now we just label the timeframe without specific dates. And we consider each period as a timeframe, rather than a single date. For example, "book launch" is a period of about five weeks, rather than the one specific day the book goes live on Amazon.

In your marketing strategy you will have noted everything you'll need to do to market your book, yourself as an author, and perhaps your business. To start filling in your tactical timeline, go back through your marketing strategy and highlight every activity, every to-do, and move it over to the appropriate group based on which objective it will help you achieve and which timeframe it needs to be done in.

This is a tool that you're going to refer to on a daily or at least weekly basis. At the beginning of every week, extract what you need to do that week and add it to your calendar, whether it's a handwritten calendar, Franklin Covey planner, Gmail or Outlook or similar calendar. Just week by week. Don't fill it out it too far into the future because things change all the time.

Contact Lists

Your contact lists are — as you might guess — a list of the people that you're going to reach out to related to your marketing activities.

Why Bother?

Putting together contact lists isn't the most fun activity, granted. However, it removes a barrier to action. (Notice a theme here?) It also helps you put your eyeballs and brain on the name of every person and think of them through the lens of your book marketing activities. It might trigger some additional thoughts, for example about their network, and give you some other ideas for how you might connect with them to help them out while at the same time furthering your own objectives. Pulling together your contact list removes a barrier to action. And that means that you're helping to set yourself up for success.

How to Assemble Your Contact Lists

Carve out a day or so to put together your contact lists. It really doesn't take much longer than a day and you can probably do it in a few hours.

Start with a review, once again, of the marketing objectives you established back in chapter 2, *Your Objectives*. Once again, skim through your whole plan and think about who you need to reach out to in order to get it all done. Pull this information together in a list.

This exercise is going to involve online research. Let's go back to the example of wanting to secure gigs as a speaker. You'll know, based on your objectives and the subject matter of your book and your genre, what kind of conferences or events are going to make sense for you to target. Research those by geography, timeline, industry, and topic. Find out who the appropriate contact person is, find their email address, phone number, Twitter handle, LinkedIn profile, and their other social media handles and build your list. Don't start calling them right away, because you won't be ready with your script and messaging yet. This step is all about getting organized so that you can be in control of your activities and do the right thing at the right time with the right information.

Don't forget your personal contact list of family and friends. I've heard stories about authors who plan the most wonderful book launch event. Everything is in place. Then the night before, they realize they've forgotten to invite the spouse's side of the family. Or the people you used to work with (before you became a full-time author or started your own business). You'll avoid this mistake when you make a concerted effort to pull together your entire list in advance.

(Media is another one of the lists, but we covered that in chapter 11, *Public Relations*.)

If you're not sure what else you should be researching, brainstorm. Bring somebody into this exercise with you and talk about what kinds of people you might need to get on your lists for outreach. In fact, when you're working through this marketing strategy, it's really helpful to engage with someone who can be a sounding board and make suggestions. Even if it's just so you can float ideas, ask questions, and solicit feedback, having someone with you can help.

I have learned from experience that it's tempting to hire somebody from one of the regions of the globe where our dollar is worth a lot more and you can get some research help for $8 an hour. Very tempting. However, if they miss the strategic connection to your objectives, you're going to get back a list that has nothing to do with what you're trying to accomplish. If you have a great virtual assistant who knows you, your business, and your book, that's fine. Do get help, bring somebody in to bounce ideas around, but make sure that they understand the strategic side of what you're actually trying to accomplish.

21

Measurement and Metrics

Measurement and metrics are how you know whether you're achieving your objectives and whether you're on your way to getting to where you want to go. You'll want to measure changes in your social media followers, website traffic, reader reviews, responses to personal outreach, clicks on the links to free downloads you've included in your book, book sales, and how much money you're spending on marketing.

Why Worry About Metrics?

You want to set up a system and process to measure metrics related to your book marketing activities because this is what tells you whether what you're doing is working. It tells you whether you need to change course or keep doing more of what you've been doing.

How to Set Up Your Dashboard

There are all kinds of tools – some sophisticated, some simple – for handling measurement and metrics. Do what works for you.

I'd suggest an Excel spreadsheet, but it doesn't even have to be that. What is important is that you start with the baseline information.

- How many website visitors are you getting?
- How many social media followers and likes are you getting?
- What's the number of book reviews that you have, and how many are five-star, four-star, three-star?
- What's your Amazon sales rank, and how many sales?
- How many pitches did you make to media and how many media stories have you been featured in?
- How many speaking engagements did you get booked for?
- How many books did you sell after each speaking engagement?
- How many clicks on the free download link you've included in your book? How about the one(s) on your website?
- How many opens and link clicks in your emails?

Use the relevant pieces of measurement and metrics that make sense for the objectives you've set for you as the author and for your book. Update the information weekly, or at least monthly.

22

Book Overview

Yes, it's finally time to create your book overview. It's the item that appears first in your marketing strategy, but you'll know by now you don't actually begin working on it until you've finished the rest of the plan.

Your book overview is a third-person description of your book, your audience, and why you, as the author, are uniquely positioned to bring this book to the reader.

Don't I Know My Book Well Enough Already?

We have had authors say to us, *"I don't need to do the book overview. I already know everything about my book."*

We quickly disabuse them of the notion that it's not required. Here's why.

The book overview helps you think about your book the way a third party would. When you're engaged in marketing, especially marketing your book, you have to be able to get into the heads of your audience members, whether it's your reader or someone else you're trying to convince to take an action. That action might be to hire you to speak at a conference or bring your books into their store. The book overview really helps you to do that.

The other reason to write a book overview from the perspective of this third party is that it provides excellent copy/paste material, making it really easy when you're doing outreach. You'll be surprised at how often you'll get a query about your book from a friend, family member, library, bookstore owner, or conference organizer, and you'll realize you have just the thing. Copy, paste, and off it goes. It's done.

How to Write Your Book Overview

You can *start* with your Amazon sales page copy, but the book overview is *not* the same as your Amazon sales copy. Your Amazon sales copy is very specifically designed to convince a potential reader to buy the book. Of course, that's what the marketing strategy is trying to help you do, but it's less direct.

The book overview for your marketing strategy needs to be a little broader than your Amazon sales copy. You are doing much more than trying to sell the book to potential readers.

Imagine yourself in a conversation with a potential literary agent, for example. What they want to know about your book is quite different from what potential readers want to learn through your Amazon sales copy. The literary agent wants to focus more on the business potential. In other words, while your Amazon sales copy is designed for potential readers, the book overview in your marketing strategy is designed for people who might help you to get the word out. I call these your influencers.

You want your book overview to answer these questions:

- What does a marketer need to know?
- What do the media need to know?
- What does an event or conference organizer need to know?

- And, perhaps, what does a bookstore owner need to know?

Then, you'll review your objectives to be sure they're appropriately reflected.

Here are some examples. As you review these, pay attention to how these book overviews differ from what you would expect to see in Amazon sales page copy.

Here's the first example:

> *This Sample Book* by Jane Author is a guide for those who find themselves responsible for job design in their workplace and for those responsible for the productivity and health of their organizations. The book offers insights into the importance of effective job design and the surprising costs of continuing to accept poorly designed and drafted job descriptions. It lays out sound strategies for becoming a job description designer, which in turn will enhance the effectiveness and function of the employees who have a much clearer idea of the details surrounding their roles.
> In today's ever-changing and fast-paced work environments, influenced by technology and an overemphasis on technical skills, the **people side** of business is neglected. It's this people side that takes care of planning and completing projects, that comes together to achieve objectives, and that, if ignored or discounted, can destroy workplace culture, contribute to the high cost of employee turnover, and undermine success.
> With the right job design, people can showcase their talents and expertise, perform well, and

feel engaged in work that matters to them. Most organizational functions overlap and intersect. Employees work as a system, not in isolation. Great job design takes this into account, from the organization-wide view to the specific tasks of a specific role and can actually generate creativity and innovation.

This Sample Book begins by exploring the knowledge fundamentals that must be in place before HR professionals, managers, and leaders can contribute to good job design. It sets out the five pillars that are the foundation for every effective job description: the purpose, scope, collaborations, reporting and managing, and results. It explores how bringing the right mindset to job design and the drafting of the job description help to prevent and manage dysfunction.

Jane Author is founder of the HR consulting firm Jane's Jobs. Having facilitated and trained HR professionals around the globe for over two decades, Jane is a respected authority in the field of job design. She works with leaders in private industry and the public sector and helps them focus on how to create organizational effectiveness through their approach to job design.

This example lets us discuss why a book overview in a book marketing strategy is not the same, and shouldn't be the same, as the Amazon sales page copy.

Right off the top the overview states that the book is a guide for those who find themselves responsible for job design in their workplace and for those responsible for the productivity and health of their organizations.

That's a good start to the book overview statement for a marketing strategy, but it would not work as well for the Amazon sales page. On your Amazon sales page you'd want to get right into the hell-versus-heaven situation your reader is in and outline how your book will help them move from the problems they're experiencing now (hell) into the post-solution world reading your book will help them attain (heaven).

The book overview is about how you, your book and its contents might solve a problem and address a business need: conference organizers want engaging content relevant to their audiences; bookstore owners want to bring in books that will resonate with their readers and they need help with how to market and place your book, and so on.

Let's look at another example from *Love You Always*, a memoir in progress at the time of this writing.

> *Love You Always* (working title) is a co-authored memoir about the emotional, practical, and experiential journeys of two mothers, each with an adult child who came out to them as transgender: one as MTF and the other as FTM. The women had been friends and neighbours for years prior to their unique shared experience with the issues faced by the transgender person, their families, friends, and community.
>
> While the book recounts at least pieces of the journey each adult child had taken as they transitioned to their alternate gender, its power is in the revelations of the vulnerability and strength found in the deeply personal stories of the moms. *Love You Always* provides poignant detail of how they found their way through a wide array of emotions – from shock, grief, fear and loneliness and

finally to understanding, hope, acceptance and joy.

By presenting practical as well as emotional stories that readers can relate to, the authors encourage friends, family, supporters, caregivers and service providers to accept and embrace the change and in turn provide the support that is so critical.

One of the authors writes under her own name, and the other is choosing to use a pen name. This illustrates how dramatically different these experiences are and can be, while grounded in the same triggering event: a transgender adult child coming out. MaryRose's story involves a mother and FTM trans son who are both comfortable with sharing their stories widely, advocating for the rights, acceptance, and equality regardless of gender identity. Gayle's story, in contrast, involves a deeply private MTF transgender daughter, her wishes to remain private, and her family's preference for continued anonymity. In a sense, this is two memoirs in one and two voices, which highlights the fact that no two journeys are the same, no matter how similar the circumstances may seem at first blush.

Again, you can see that this book overview is not the same as what you'd want to write for your Amazon sales description.

It's perfectly acceptable to use the Amazon copy as a starting point, if you've in fact written that first. It's better, though, to write your Amazon copy *after* you've completed your marketing strategy. This is because your marketing strategy will give you a better idea of who and what to focus on for your sales copy.

Once you've completed your book overview, put it away for a little bit, and then come back to it with the list of questions laid out earlier. You want to connect the audiences – marketer, media, bookstores, conference organizers, and so on – with the results promised by your book, helping them see what's in it for them.

Strategy Brief

Your strategy brief summarizes the audience, the reader, and what they'll get out of the book. It articulates a high-level summary, in one or two sentences, of what your book marketing approach is. It's like an elevator pitch, which is a brief explanation of the idea, product (e.g. your book), or company. On my first job as a reporter, I had to learn pretty quickly how to pitch story ideas to my news director in twenty-five words or less. That was an elevator pitch. The name — elevator pitch — reflects the notion that you should be able to deliver the summary in the time span of a thirty-second to two-minute elevator ride.

Like the book overview, you're don't write the brief until you've finished the rest of your strategy.

Why Write a Strategy Brief?

You might be tempted to skip doing the strategy brief because you think you know what's going on. Many authors feel the same. Don't be like them. The reasons you'll want to craft a strategy brief include that it helps you think, um, strategically about your book marketing approach. It's like the walls and the roof of your plan.

How to Write Your Brief

You've done all the work on the details. Now you need to exercise that strategic part of your brain, raise yourself back out and summarize what your book marketing strategy is all about. If you can do that, you'll find it easier to pitch your story too.

You'll summarize the reader, what the book will do for them, your objectives and your tactical approaches. But the strategy brief is two paragraphs at the most.

On to an example.

> *This Sample Book* will resonate with readers and leaders who want to make a significant contribution to enhancing organizational effectiveness through sophisticated job design. It targets those who want to lead by example, who value their employees as human beings, and who understand that a healthy bottom line exists because of people, not in spite of them. This Sample Book offers practical wisdom for making their workplace better.
>
> This strategy lays out a multi-pronged approach to address the three interrelated objectives of raising awareness, generating speaking engagements, and encouraging book sales. Jane Author will be positioned as a mentor and thought leader. On social media, LinkedIn and Twitter will be key platforms. We'll leverage existing contacts and network, employ public relations outreach to garner media attention, proactively cultivate new invitations to deliver speeches and training

sessions, and refresh and update the author website.

In the above example, the first paragraph is the summary of who the reader/s are.

- Who will this book resonate with? The target audience and reader are those *who want to make a significant contribution to enhancing organizational effectiveness through sophisticated job design.*
- Why is it going to resonate with them and what is it going to do for them? It offers *practical wisdom for making their workplace better.*
- What is the strategy going to involve? It's going to involve positioning the author *as a mentor and thought leader*; it's going to involve social media, PR and media outreach, a refreshed website, and attempts to secure speaking and training engagements.

24

Pulling It All Together

Finally, it's time to pull it all together. Build yourself a shell template for your strategy, in Microsoft Word, Google Docs, or Pages. Include the categories we've talked about so far where you know you're going to want to be active. As a model, use the sample completed marketing strategy you'll find access to at the back of this book.

Keep doing your research, write it down, cross check your messages with your methods and other tactics, and ensure you've included all potential costs in your budget.

Be sure to format your marketing strategy so it looks beautifully professional. You may be tempted to just leave it messy and leave it in a working state. Don't do that. A well-done marketing strategy that's formatted and looks beautiful is all of a sudden another tool you can leverage in your marketing efforts. For instance, if you're out at a conference and you meet an agent or a publisher who's looking to take on a book like yours, or another conference organizer looking for speakers, all you have to do is whip out your beautiful, well-thought-out, complete marketing strategy, and you'll have a convert.

So finish it, make it beautiful, print a few copies at your local print shop and ask them to add front and back covers in clear plastic or your favourite colour and hold it together with cerlox or coil binding. Keep some copies on your desk and carry one or two with you, along with your other promotional materials. Keep it visible for yourself and, of course, save the electronic version. Use it as a reference guide to everything you're doing related to the marketing of your book.

Afterword

By now you will have a good idea what's involved with creating your own book marketing strategy. And you'll have confidence you have what it takes to pull together the plan that will land you firmly in the drivers' seat of your author and business career.

By adopting this approach to your marketing strategy, you'll learn much more about the market into which you are launching your book, and you'll actually learn more about your book and its audiences.

You'll be better equipped to deal with the challenge of volume. It's true there is so much that it is *possible to do*, but you'll now see that you can cut through the clutter by aligning what you will *actually do* with the objectives you want to achieve with your marketing.

The only way to get a handle on which of the gazillion possible things to do, and what is right for you and *your* book, is to craft your own marketing strategy. You'll end up with a clear understanding of what to do, when, and why.

Did You Get Your Free Companion Workbook?

To help you get started with your book marketing strategy, I'm offering a free companion workbook that you can use to develop your own book marketing strategy.

Download the free workbook by clicking this link, or by copying/pasting/typing it into your browser:

https://ingeniumbooks.com/one-million-readers-workbook/

To obtain a completed nonfiction marketing strategy you can use as a guide, along with this book, in support of you crafting your own book marketing strategy, proceed to https://ingeniumbooks.com/one-million-readers-sample-strategy/ .

Like all other authors, reviews make my world go round. If you feel so inclined, please consider leaving an honest review where you bought the book. I would be forever grateful.

Acknowledgments

This book wouldn't be possible without the authors who afforded me and Ingenium Books the privilege of working on marketing strategies for their nonfiction books. You know who you are.

Thanks also to the team here at Ingenium Books, including: Molly Billings, Trina Holt, and Doug Murray. We developed our approach to book marketing strategies together, hands on, and in real time.

For letting me know there was a demand for this material by requesting a video webinar, I thank Tahlia Newland, Ken Decroo, Susan Welch, Lyn Behan, Kirk Sowers, Gary Kreigh, David Kerr, and William Sandberg.

For reading early versions of the manuscript and providing excellent feedback, heartfelt thanks go to Marie Beswick Arthur, Maureen Fisher, Ladey Adey, Christine Smeeth, Alice Briggs, and Linell van Hoepen. I'd also like to thank the Alliance of Independent Authors for being such a fantastic resource for so many independent authors, and Orna Ross for the nudging influence to put writing my own books in a priority position every day.

And finally, to my husband and business partner John, for being there to encourage, support, organize, provide feedback and sober second thought to all my crazy ideas.

About the Author

Boni Wagner-Stafford is co-founder of Ingenium Books, where the purpose is *breathing life into ideas*. Ingenium Books does this by helping professional entrepreneurs overcome the three major roadblocks that stop authors from publishing their book: time, expertise, and marketing.

Boni is a writer, ghostwriter, and editor specializing in nonfiction. She also coaches nonfiction authors writing their own books in the genres of business, self-help, personal development, memoir, and journalistic nonfiction.

As an award-winning former Canadian journalist (under the names Boni Fox and Boni Fox Gray), Boni covered politics, government, social and economic policy, health care, and organized crime. She also held senior management roles in government where she led teams responsible for media relations, issues management, and strategic communications planning.

As an entrepreneur, Boni has muddied her hands in the trenches with one-page strategic plans, cash flow forecasts, developing purpose and core values, franchise structures, sales targets, and marketing and differentiation.

Boni has been at the controls of a helicopter, canoed in the wild backcountry of Northern Ontario, jumped out of an airplane, sang on stage with Andrea Bocelli and Christopher Plummer (not at the same time), and grew up skiing in the Rocky Mountains. She has lived in seventeen different cities/towns in Canada, Mexico and France.

Other books by Boni

Rock Your Business: 26 Essential Lessons to Start, Run, and Grow Your New Business from the Ground Up

(with John Wagner-Stafford)

Kitty Karma: Big Stories of the Small Cats Who Change Our Lives

(editor and contributing author)

Wanted: How to Create a Relationship that Really Works

(editor)

No More Author Envy: 9 Essential Steps to Writing Your First Book

www.ingramcontent.com/pod-product-compliance
Lightning Source LLC
Chambersburg PA
CBHW071853070526
44583CB00016B/1666